A SLIGHTLY CYNICAL HISTORY
OF AMERICAN JEWS

LOUIS BRANDEIS SLEPT HERE

A SLIGHTLY CYNICAL HISTORY
OF AMERICAN JEWS

by

David Gleicher

gefen
publishing house

Typesetting: Marzel A.S. – Jerusalem

Cover Design: Gil Friedman / Gefen

Edition 9 8 7 6 5 4 3 2

Gefen Publishing House Ltd.   Gefen Books
POB 36004, Jerusalem   12 New St., Hewlett
91360 Israel   N.Y., U.S.A. 11557
972-2-5380247   516-295-2805

Printed in Israel
Send for our free catalogue

Library of Congress Cataloging-in-Publication Data
Gleicher, David, 1954-
Louis Brandeis Slept Here: a slightly cynical history of american jews / by David Gleicher.
    p.   cm.
ISBN: 965-229-167-6
1. Jews—United States—History—Humor. 2. United States—Ethnic relations—Humor. I. Title.
E184.J5G538 1997
973'.04924—dc20
                                                    96-36479
                                                    CIP

CONTENTS

To Ruth,

*Who proved that even a biologist
can appreciate history
when it's presented well.*

ACKNOWLEDGMENTS

I was first hired to lecture on American Jewish history by Leah Polin, executive director of the Dawn Schuman Institute for Jewish Learning. When Leah asked who my lecturing role model was, I answered, Jay Leno. Despite (or because of) that, Leah has, through the years, spread my name as a speaker throughout the greater Chicago area, and I thank her for all her help.

My interest in history is derived from the experiences of my parents, Leon and Lottie Gleicher. Their stories of life in pre-war Europe and adventures in the Holocaust led to my devouring of World War II and Jewish history books at a young age, developing my love of history that has lasted until today.

My in-laws, Arnold and June Steinberg, have always supported my various endeavors. In the case of "Louis Brandeis," that support was moral, financial, and, in my mother-in-law's case, editorial as well.

My wife, Ruth, teaches biology at Niles West High School and Ida Crown Jewish Academy. As a non-historian, she was my sounding-board for this book. When Ruth gave it thumbs up, I felt I had succeeded in writing the type of work that would be the Jewish version of the Davis and Shenkman books that I mention in the Preface.

My final thanks goes to someone who will never read this book. Rabbi Louis Bernstein was my original American Jewish history teacher, first at Camp Massad, later at Yeshiva University. As the head of many Jewish organizations throughout his life, "Louie" was the personification of a community "leader," yet, with all that, he remained an unpretentious man of the people. His *Ahavat Yisrael* led to his having excellent personal relationships with most of his colleagues, even those with whom he disagreed politically and philosophically. He died in 1995 at the age of 67, leaving behind thousands of students, colleagues and congregants whom he had influenced in so many ways.

Preface

I love history. When it's taught well or written well, history is as fascinating as any TV mini-series; filled with heroes and villains, drama and suspense, triumph and tragedy. Unfortunately, much of today's historical writing is done by professors addressing other professors in a dry, boring style. The reading public, however, is hungry for books that that make history come alive. Works such as "Don't Know Much About History," by Kenneth Davis and "Legends, Lies and Cherished Myths of American History," by Richard Shenkman have become best-sellers, and The History Channel has become the cable TV success story of the '90s.

The field of Jewish history suffers from the same problems as general history. With the possible exception of the works of the late Max Dimont, there has never been a popularly-written, entertaining, yet factual, history of the Jews in general, and American Jews in particular. This book aims to fill that gap.

"Louis Brandeis Slept Here" traces the history of American Jews from the community's origin in 1654 until today. This book is a modified version of a series of lectures I've delivered over the years on American Jewish history. As in my lectures, the book is peppered with cynicism, humor, and snide remarks (usually hidden in the footnotes). While my comments place "Louis Brandeis" close to the spirit of the hysterical best-seller, "Dave Barry Slept Here," this book, unlike Barry's, remains rooted in historical reality.

The author who had the most influence on the style and tone of this book is Richard Armour. His history of America, "It All Started With Columbus," is the best of Armour's many off-center, humorous books on history and other academic topics. His books are out-of-print, but can be found in most libraries.

I realize that there are many people and events that I have left out of this book. "Louis Brandeis," however, is an introduction. It is meant not only to inform, but also to pique your interest. If any part of this chronicle makes you want to explore further an aspect of American Jewish history, simply refer to the annotated bibliography, where I have placed all my sources.

The spirit of cynicism, sarcasm, and skepticism that permeates this book is the result of my being both the son of Holocaust survivors and a criminal defense attorney. In fact, Chapter 3 was written during a two-month multi-defendant crack conspiracy trial, a proceeding that included lying witnesses and corrupt DEA agents – and those were the government's people. It's no wonder that I have a cynical skeptical nature. However, "Louis Brandeis" adds humor and irreverence to the cynicism to keep the history from becoming downbeat. As the subtitle says, this book is only "slightly" cynical.

So sit back, relax, and learn how American Jews got to where they are today, and where they may be headed tomorrow.

INTRODUCTION

Let's begin with a global question: How did most of America's Jews get here? Two thousand years ago, almost half the world's 8 million or so Jews[1] lived in Judea.[2] In 70 C.E., Judea lost its war of rebellion against the Roman Army.[3] Many Jews ended up in Rome as POWs, joining the century-old Roman Jewish community.

Eventually, Rome fell to the Barbarian hordes, and Europe entered the uncivilized Dark Ages (as opposed to the more civilized Europe of the 1940s). The Jews moved north, from Rome to Northern Italy, up the Rhine to Franco-Germany. Under Charlemagne (800), Jews were welcomed, but after the pogroms of the First Crusade (1096), the situation went downhill. Jews started moving east, to Poland, especially after the Black Death in 1348, when Jews were accused of poisoning the wells. Jews spent the next several centuries in Eastern Europe, until moving en masse to America, beginning in the 1880s.

And that's how most Jews came to America from their ancestral Biblical homeland. Now, on to the details.

---

1. Talk about zero population growth. In 2,000 years, the world's Jewish population has gone from 8 million to about 12 million.
2. Even 2,000 years ago, most Jews lived outside of Israel, but sent donations to the Temple in Jerusalem. This system has since been replaced by Israel Bonds.
3. That's what you call the Italian Army when it defeats you in battle.

CHAPTER 1

COLONIAL AMERICA

The First Jews, Or There Goes the Neighborhood

The majority of the Jews in 17th Century America were Sephardim, descendants of Jews expelled from Spain in 1492. First, some background:

Jews had lived in Spain for over 1,000 years. In the 14th century, their position began to deteriorate until the final expulsion on August 2, 1492. Many Jews found it impossible to leave their homeland, and, in order to stay, converted to Catholicism. From 1391 through 1492, over 200,000 Jews became "New Christians," also known as "Marranos."

Many of these Marranos, especially those in Portugal, were Catholics by compulsion, and practiced Judaism in secret. They lived in fear of the Inquisition, which used torture to uncover "Judaizers."[1] Miraculously, many Marranos were able to stick to their secret beliefs for over a century. In the 1500s, after Holland had achieved independence, Marranos fled there. In the liberal atmosphere of Amsterdam, the Marranos came out of

---

1. Tragically, some secret Jews were uncovered when, rather than placing money in the church collection plate, they announced a pledge of 10 pesos instead.

the closet, and embraced their ancestral religion. Other Sephardim moved to England after Oliver Cromwell opened the doors in 1656.

Some Sephardic Jews, perhaps because they were less rooted than their Gentile neighbors, become pioneers in the New World. Holland had captured the city of Recife in Brazil from the Portuguese in the 1600s. By 1645, Recife had 1,000 Jews, two synagogues,[1] a school, and the Western Hemisphere's first rabbi. In 1654, that world came to an end when Portugal recaptured Recife. The generous Portuguese graciously allowed the Jews to stay – **if** they converted to Catholicism. Most of the Recife Jews knew of Iberian hospitality first-hand, and declined the offer.

Once again, a Jewish community was on the move, this time back to Holland. However, 23 Jews (4 men, 6 women, and 13 young people), who had boarded the St. Catherine, ended up going north instead of east.[2] On September 1, 1654,[3] the 23 landed in New Amsterdam, New Amsterdam (now called, of course, New York, New York). This marks the official beginning of the Jewish community of the United States.

It wasn't such a good beginning. The captain of the St. Catherine, a rude Frenchman[4] named De La Motte, claimed the passengers still owed him for their fare (which was expensive because their tickets had not been purchased at least seven days in advance). De La Motte had their belongings sold at auction to pay the bill owed. Fortunately, two Jewish merchants, Jacob Barsimson and Solomon Peterson, had been in New Amsterdam at the time, and helped their co-religionists get settled.

The governor of New Amsterdam, Peter Stuyvesant, didn't like Jews very much. Some years before, when he had been governor of Curacao, some Jewish settlers arrived. Stuyvesant was under the impression that they had come to be farmers; instead, they became store-owners and

---

1. One they prayed in, and the other, they wouldn't be caught dead in.
2. To use a Yiddish term, they were "fahrblunjet."
3. We're not sure of the exact date in September, but September 1, 1654 is easy to remember.
4. Now there's a tautology.

merchants (big surprise!). Stuyvesant thought he'd been lied to, and disliked Jews ever after.

But Stuyvesant wasn't merely anti-Semitic; he hated everyone – at least everyone who wasn't a member of the Dutch Reformed Church. Even in 1654, New Amsterdam was made up of many nationalities, none of whom Stuyvesant liked. In addition, his leg had been blown off in battle. Prosthetics not being very advanced, Stuyvesant was forced to walk painfully on a pegleg. All this contributed to Peter Stuyvesant's being a very grouchy fellow.

When the Jews arrived, Stuyvesant wrote to his bosses at the Dutch West India Company (the real rulers of New Amsterdam), asking to get rid of these people, known for "their customary usury and deceitful trading with Christians." The Jews wrote their own letter in their defense. The Company's Jewish stockholders, upon receiving the letters, asked their non-Jewish compatriots to turn down the governor's request. In February, 1655, the Company ordered Stuyvesant to let the Jews stay, as long as they didn't become "public charges" (that is, go on welfare).

Stuyvesant was unhappy, but persistent. Some of the newcomers, led by Asher Levy, wanted to serve on the local militia. Stuyvesant said no; pay a tax instead. Levy cried foul, and dashed off another letter to Amsterdam. Again, the Jewish stockholders spoke to their friends, and Stuyvesant lost, though this time, New Amsterdam's fear of Indian attacks might have played a role in the decision.

Later, Jews requested the right to trade further in the Dutch territory away from New Amsterdam. Stuyvesant said no. Another letter was sent. The Company harshly told Stuyvesant that it was sick and tired of all these letters, that he should get along with the Jewish settlers. Otherwise, the Jewish stockholders would continue to "noodge" (pester) their non-Jewish friends, making everyone unhappy.

Stuyvesant finally got the message, and left the Jews alone. In fact, in 1657, the Jews were given "burgher" rights, that is, the right to sell goods at retail (there's a joke there somewhere).

Despite all this uproar about their rights, the Jewish population of New Amsterdam never numbered more than 50.[1] In fact, the town lost its Jewish settlers to such an extent that in 1663 the community sent its Torah scroll back to Holland; there weren't enough Jews in New Amsterdam to warrant having it.

Where were all the Jews of the New World? In those days, the center of the Jewish community in America was in the Caribbean: Curacao, Barbados, and other islands were the population centers. In those days, Jews were smart. They said, who wants to live where it's so cold. Curacao is sunny and warm all year round; New Amsterdam is cold in the winter, and humid in the summer. It took 300 years before the Jews of America regained their senses, and, in homage to their past, headed for Miami Beach.

In 1664, the British captured New Amsterdam, and changed its name to New York.[2] By then, the only Jew around to sign the oath of allegiance to England was Asher Levy. Under the British, New York's Jewish population increased, growing to 100 by 1700. Levy was the de facto head of the community until his death in 1682. He practiced about a dozen different professions, including merchant, butcher, and fur trader. Levy was well-known outside of New York as well. When a Jewish peddler was fined in New England, Levy spoke up for the man, and the fine was removed – out of respect for Levy.

Levy served on a jury in a civil suit involving his old enemy, Peter Stuyvesant. Rather than using the occasion to seek revenge, Levy remained objective, and Stuyvesant even won the case. It is not known if Stuyvesant's opinion of Jews changed after that.

---

1. Historians have discovered that, despite their small numbers, these Jews were constantly fighting with each other, thus setting an example that the American Jewish community has followed ever since.
2. Thank goodness for that. Can you imagine Frank Sinatra singing "It's up to you, New Amsterdam, New Amsterdam"?

In today's Manhattan, Stuyvesant has the last word. The governor has a prestigious high school named after him. A few blocks away, Asher Levy has only an elementary school bearing his name.

Social and Cultural Life

One of the first items of business for the 23 Jewish settlers in 1654 was to organize a synagogue, which they called Shearith Israel (Remnant of Israel). I always get a thrill out of Shearith Israel's little ad in the Friday New York Times' synagogue services section: It says "Shearith Israel – The Spanish-Portuguese Synagogue, Founded 1654." That ad tells America's WASP elite, "We've been here as long as you – if not earlier."

Services were held in private homes, then in rented quarters. In 1730, with about 250 Jews in New York, Shearith Israel moved into its first building.[1] It has since moved several times, and is located today at Central Park West and 70th Street on Manhattan's Upper West Side. Besides a synagogue building, the community also built a mikveh (ritual bath) and, each autumn, a communal succah.

Jews kept coming to America in a small, but steady stream. Many Jews in Europe were very poor (over 1/2 of London's Jews lived in poverty). They figured that they might as well try their luck in the New World. By the mid-1700s, there were six other synagogues in America: In Newport, Philadelphia, Lancaster (Pa.), Richmond, Charleston, and Savannah. All these synagogues followed the Sephardi (Spanish) ritual. However, the majority of American Jews since the 1730s were Ashkenazim (European, primarily German).

So why were all the synagogues still Sephardic? The Sephardim were here first. When the Ashkenazic newcomers arrived, they wanted to be "Americans," and the "American" form of Judaism was Sephardic.

---

1. That building no longer exists. The oldest synagogue building in the U.S. is the "Touro Synagogue" in Newport. The oldest synagogue building in the Western Hemisphere, in Curacao, is a major tourist attraction there.

Therefore, because Sephardic = American, the Ashkenazim all adopted the Sephardi ritual.[1] In America, unlike Europe and the Caribbean, where Sephardim exhibited arrogant hostility towards Ashkenazim, the two groups got along just fine. Intermarriage between them, however, took longer. In 1740, when Sephardi Isaac Seixas (pronounced "Say-shess") married Ashkenazi Rachel Levy, most of the groom's side failed to show up. It took Seixas years to forgive his family for this insult. Yet, this Seixas-Levy union produced the great leader of early American Jewry, Gershom Mendes Seixas (more on him later).

In those days – in fact, not until 1840 – there were no ordained rabbis in America. Synagogues were led by a "Hazzan" (literally, cantor) or minister, who served as a lay rabbi. While not as knowledgeable as European rabbis, the hazzanim made their contributions to American Judaism. It was Hazzan Isaac Pinto who, in 1761, published the first translation of the High Holiday machzor into English.

Each synagogue was run by its parnas (president) and its board of trustees, not by the hazzan (some things never change, even after three centuries). The board would institute a whole schedule of fines for various offenses: Working on the Sabbath – $5.00; shaving on the Sabbath – $1.00;[2] sleeping during the services – $.25,[3] etc. The level of enforcement of the fines depended on how powerful the board was. Eventually, the fines system disappeared. Interestingly, one of colonial Jewry's greatest problems was finding candidates to serve as parnas. The job was time-consuming, required the possible disciplining of friends and relatives, and, in America, had no real power.

Even in colonial times, American Jews tried to help their co-religionists around the world. In the 1770s, Rabbi Hayim Isaac Carigal of Hebron came

---

1. Unfortunately, they didn't also adopt those great Sephardic names like Gomez, Lopez, Pardo, etc. If they had, their descendants could have taken advantage of the many affirmative action programs reserved for Hispanics.
2. If your face was naturally smooth, you were in trouble.
3. There being no regular boring Sabbath sermons in those days, there was no excuse for sleeping.

to the colonies to raise money for his community. Rabbi Carigal was received with much enthusiasm by American Jews, especially in Newport. On May 28, 1773, he delivered a sermon to the congregation during the Shavuot[1] services. His sermon was attended by high-ranking Rhode Island officials as well as the future president of Yale. All were suitably impressed. Some of the American congregations asked Carigal to remain as their rabbi, but he turned them all down. No fool, he accepted an offer in sunny Barbados, but unfortunately died young before he could have any impact in the New World.

The reception given Rabbi Carigal notwithstanding, colonial American Jewry had little or no interest in Jewish learning. The founders of the College of Rhode Island (now, Brown University) offered the Newport Jewish community the opportunity to establish a chair of Jewish studies. The community contributed to the new college, but said no thanks to the Jewish studies idea.

Colonial Jews were interested in business and economics, not learning and liberal arts. While that flies against the majority trend among Jews today, that attitude can still be found in Brooklyn's Syrian-Jewish community. Most Syrians are involved in business, not the professions, humanities, or social sciences. In that respect, they resemble the colonial community.

Why weren't colonial American Jews in those "Jewish" professions, medicine and law? Medicine was not a lucrative field in those days (and 18th century doctors couldn't blame HMOs and managed care either). As for law, to quote one historian, "Lawyers were in bad repute throughout much of this period." (So nothing's changed.) In those days, Jewish mothers kvelled (bragged) over, "My son, the merchant."

American Jewish historian Jacob Marcus described the vocation of the average American Jew on the eve of the Revolution: "An urban shopkeeper of German ancestry, firmly, proudly, and nostalgically rooted in his religious tradition."

---

1. Shavuot: Winner of the award for Least Known Major Holiday Among American Jews.

The Eve of Revolution or Erev Revolution

In 1776, there were 1500-2500 Jews in the colonies out of a total population of 2½ million, less than 1/10 of one percent. That's the equivalent of a Jewish population in today's America of only 250,000.

Even before independence, America was the best land in the world for the Jews. Compared to Europe, it was virtually free of anti-Semitic prejudice. Why was America different? First, it had lots of land, but few people. Americans couldn't afford to be prejudiced – they needed settlers too badly. Also, most Americans left Europe to be free of its prejudices; anti-Semitism could be viewed as a European idea.

In addition, colonial America was a polyglot society. There is a myth that Americans of that period all looked and spoke like George Bush (or any generic TV anchorman). That's just not so. I'll quote Marcus again:

"In a society of Dunkers, Congregationalists, Moravian Brethren, Baptists, Christian Sabbatarians, Catholics, Methodists, Anglicans, Presbyterians (Old Side and New Side), Lutherans, Dutch Reformed, German Reformed, Mennonites, Schwenkfelders, a society of English, Scottish, Irish, German, Dutch, Welsh, Swiss, and Swedish settlers – not to mention Negroes[1] and Indians – the Jew did not stand out too conspicuously."

That point was especially true because colonial Jews, unlike their Eastern European brethren, dressed like their neighbors, further making them part of American society. It was not uncommon for Jewish merchants to form business partnerships with non-Jews, an extremely rare situation in Europe.

All this did not mean that colonial American Jews were assimilationists. They tried to keep the mitzvot (commandments) as best they could. One of America's wealthiest Jews, Newport shipping magnate, Aaron Lopez, not only conducted no business on the Sabbath, but refused to allow any of his ships to leave port on Saturdays as well. Michael Gratz

---

1. Don't fault Marcus here. He wrote this long before Negroes became Blacks, much less African-Americans.

is another example of a merchant who would stop all business in order to keep the Sabbath, even when he was traveling or trading in the western wilderness (today's central Pennsylvania). His non-Jewish partner, William Murray, would mutter and sputter about it, but Gratz stayed true to his beliefs.

Some members of the community got involved in the kosher food business, exporting ritually slaughtered meat to the Caribbean. In 1757, New York merchants had to respond to charges that meat they had sold to Jamaica and Curacao wasn't kosher. The New Yorkers strongly denied the allegations. This early argument over kashrut set a pattern in American Jewish life that continues until today.

The Revolution or The Spirit of 5536[1]

Early American Jewish historians looked far and wide for American Jews who had participated in the Revolutionary War. They found about 50 veterans. Ironically, it is the more professional historians who have uncovered even more participants, for a total of about 100. If 2500 Jews lived in the Colonies, those 100 patriots are the equivalent of 220,000 Jewish soldiers today.

An American myth is that most of the Colonists were supporters of the Revolution. Sorry, but no. One-third of the people were revolutionaries, 1/3 were Loyalists, and 1/3 were waiting to see who would win (so they could say "I was with you all along."). Among Jews, the Loyalist faction existed, but in a much lower percentage (probably about 10%). Why is this? Jews had great freedom in the Colonies, but the Revolution offered the prospect of even more. Also, Jews, most of whom were of German origin, had fewer ties to "Mother England."

Three men illustrate the Jewish experience during the Revolution: The first is Francis Salvador (1747-1776), a rich kid from England, who came

---

1. Do some arithmetic. If July, 1996 fell in the Jewish year 5756, then what was the Jewish year when John Hancock signed the Declaration of Independence?

to South Carolina to oversee family holdings there. He fell in love with America and got involved in politics. In 1774, he was elected to the South Carolina House, the first Jew elected to public office in America. The popular Salvador became friends with other leaders of South Carolina. He cast his lot with the Revolution, and seemed destined for greatness. Unfortunately, in 1776, he was killed in battle against local Indians[1] who were allied with the British.

The second figure is Gershom Seixas (1746-1816), the "Patriot Rabbi of the Revolution," and one of the products of the 1740 Seixas-Levy "intermarriage." He was appointed hazzan of Shearith Israel at the age of 22, and was American Jewry's first native-born religious leader. When New York was occupied by the British in 1776, Seixas refused to remain behind in enemy territory. He left for Philadelphia, taking Shearith Israel's Torah scrolls with him.[2]

After the war, despite pleadings to stay in Philly, Seixas returned to Shearith Israel, where he remained until his death. He was greatly honored and respected in the community at large, and served as a trustee of the new Columbia College for thirty years. Seixas's own Jewish knowledge was limited; any graduate of a modern day school could probably put him to shame. However, in post-Revolutionary War America, he was the most learned leader the community had, and his total dedication to his small congregation made up for his lack of Talmudic training.

The final person is the most famous: Haym Salomon (1740-1785). Salomon was a rarity in revolutionary America – a Polish Jew. Despite that, he was elected a trustee of Philadelphia's Congregation Mikveh Israel, the lone "Poilisher" among the Sephardim and Germans.

---

1. They were promoted to "Native-Americans" in the 1980s.
2. Yet, Shearith Israel remained open and functioning. How? Among the Hessian mercenaries were Jews. One of the more knowledgeable Hessian Jews kept the synagogue open, and possibly even served as its unofficial hazzan. Many, if not most, of these Hessian Jews remained in America after the war.

Salomon's efforts on behalf of the Revolution have risen to mythic proportions (and you've seen what I do to myths). Did he single-handedly finance the Revolution with his own money? Not quite, but his contribution was crucial nonetheless.

Salomon performed two services for the new government: First, he made personal loans to patriot leaders. You don't get a steady paycheck running a revolution, and people like James Madison were running out of lunch money. Salomon gave them the funds to pay their rent and grocery bills – in other words, to survive.

The second contribution involved the actual financing of the Revolution. The Continental Congress issued bonds to raise money for the new United States. Salomon's job was to find suckers willing to invest in a brand-new government, which might or might not pay back the bondholders. Well, Salomon was a smooth talker. He found enough gamblers willing to take a chance on the Patriots (or at least cover the spread) by buying their bonds. And that's how the Revolution was financed.

Salomon was to be paid on a commission basis, and was still owed a lot of money when he died young in 1785. His heirs spent much time and effort trying to get Congress to pay the bill, but the response was, "Haym who?" The money was never paid, and Congress' reputation for honesty and reliability has remained the same until today.

After the war's end in 1783, American Jews celebrated with everyone else. In fact, the huge celebratory parade in Philadelphia even had a special kosher table.[1] Because of their contributions to the war effort, Jews felt that they were entitled to full equal civil rights. Jonas Phillips, a community leader, wrote a letter to the delegates of the Constitutional Convention in 1787, telling them, "You owe us. Make sure we get our equal rights." Unbeknownst to Phillips (because the Convention meetings were secret), the new Constitution provided for just that in Article VI

---

1. Amazingly, there is no record of any disputes regarding Jews who refused to eat because the food wasn't kosher enough.

(prohibiting religious tests for holding office) and in its Bill of Rights, specifically, the First Amendment.

But the Constitution gave the Jews equal rights only as to the federal government. The states could do as they pleased. Some states refused to follow the federal lead, and denied Jews equal rights. This could theoretically lead to absurd situations. For example, a Jew could be elected president of the United States or U.S. senator from Maryland; but a Jew could not be elected village councilman or dogcatcher in Maryland, because only Christians could hold public **state** office there. This example is not just theoretical. President Jefferson named Reuben Etting U.S. Marshall for Maryland. As a Jew, Etting could not have held any local office in that state. Maryland did not remove these restrictions until 1825; North Carolina and New Hampshire had similar laws on their books until after the Civil War.

Also important in establishing the Jews' position in the New Republic[1] was President Washington's letter to the Newport congregation in 1790. That community, as well as others, had sent Washington a congratulatory letter upon his inauguration. In his response, Washington used much of the language found in the letter he had received. The key section is the following:

"It is no more that toleration is spoken of, as if it was by the indulgence of one class of people, that another enjoyed the exercise of their inherent natural rights. For happily, the government of the United States, which gives to bigotry no sanction, to persecution no assistance, requires only that they who live under its protection should demean themselves as good citizens."

In other words, Washington was saying: This isn't Europe, where the best Jews could hope for is to be tolerated. This is America, where Jews and Gentiles have equal rights. If any bigotry or prejudice exists, it will not be supported or endorsed by the government.

---

1. That reminds me, The New Republic is an excellent magazine. I highly recommend it.

This statement was important, coming as it did from the most popular man in the country. Washington would set the tone for all aspects of the new nation, including its belief in equality.

Ironically, the Washington letter marked the last gasp of the Newport Jewish community. Their major source of income, the import-export trade, never recovered from the war, and, by 1790, the community had begun its steady decline.

Chapter 2

BEFORE THE CIVIL WAR,[1]
OR THE YEKKIES ARE COMING,
THE YEKKIES ARE COMING[2]

In 1820, the majority of American Jews were native-born (a statistic that would not be seen again until the 1950s). Why was that? No immigrants. Napoleon had given the Jews of Europe hope for the future by removing anti-Jewish laws in the countries he had conquered. After Waterloo, the reaction set in. The various German states returned to their prior oppressive selves.

In 1819, things got worse, with anti-Semitic pogroms led by German university students.[3] Many Jews saw that there was no future in Germany,[4] and, in the 1820s, the mass immigration to America began. The

---

1. Or, as historians call it, ante-bellum. In Yiddish, "der Tante Bella."
2. German Jews are called "Yekkies." Why? Even Leo Rosten, in "The Joys of Yiddish," admits he doesn't have an answer. Perhaps it comes from their propensity to be fanatically neat and clean. When they'd see dirt or an item out of place, German Jews would yell "Yek," leading to the name.
3. That should come as no surprise. In 1941, the German Einsatzgruppen (death squads) were led by theology students, lawyers, and other professional, educated people.
4. Of course, it took some Jews until 1938 to come to that conclusion.

numbers tell the story: In 1820 America had 2,700 Jews (only .03% of the American population). By 1850, that amount had increased 18-fold, to 50,000. Only ten years later, that number tripled to 150,000.

Jews weren't the only Germans who had given up on Europe. By 1880, 5 million Germans had immigrated to America; 200,000 of those Germans were Jews.

Most of the first wave of this immigration had come from Bavaria in southern Germany. Bavaria was Germany's most Catholic area, and its most anti-Semitic. In addition to the usual Jew laws, a new one was added: A marriage quota. No Jewish weddings could take place unless a space opened up on the official Jewish marriage list, called the Matrikel (and you thought rent control was tough).

Another common feature of the early German-Jewish immigrants was their status: They tended to be among the poorest and least-educated Jews. That shouldn't be surprising. The poor have the least to lose by leaving; the least-educated have the bleakest future. Interestingly, the "average" German Jew grew richer as the emigration increased because the poorest members of the community were leaving for America. (Ah statistics.)

After 1848, following the failure of democratic revolutions throughout Europe, the better-off and more-educated Jews left for America. The events of 1848 had finally crushed their hopes as well. While most Jews in the mid-19th century immigration were German, there were many Eastern Europeans among them as well. The latter, however, tended to speak German (which they thought had a higher status than Yiddish), and were thus lumped together with the Yekkies.

The new immigrants arrived in small groups of friends and relatives. There were many cases of brothers and sisters arriving together. After all, who would watch over a single Jewish girl more diligently than her big brother? Most German Jews followed a similar path to the American dream. The immigrant, knowing little English and having few resources, began by peddling, usually in rural areas. It was not an easy occupation: The peddler carried on his back a pack that could weigh up to 80 pounds;

there was always a danger of being robbed or killed; and there was a lack of community in this new and strange country which led to loneliness and depression. Despite those obstacles, Jews aspired to self-employment, and relied on family networks to get the financing to start peddling.

Success was often a matter of luck: Abraham Kohn (we'll see more of him later), fresh from Germany, tried peddling in New England. Unfortunately, his targeted customers were members of a sect that believed the messianic era would arrive any day (sort of like Christian Lubavitchers). Kohn found it hard to sell kitchen implements to people who thought the world was coming to an end.

Peddlers who were somewhat successful advanced from carrying packs on their backs to owning a horse and wagon instead. The horse and wagon evolved into a small dry goods store. Finally, the dry goods store grew into a general purpose department store. Not every peddler became Abraham & Strauss or I. Magnin or Gimbel, but most advanced beyond the horse and wagon stage.

Peddling dry goods led to Jewish control of the American clothing industry in the mid-1800s. An example of this can be seen in Cincinnati, where, in 1860, 65 out of the Queen City's 70 clothing firms were Jewish-owned.

Mordecai Manuel Noah

As in the last chapter, there are three Jews of this period whose lives are interesting enough to examine more closely. The first of these is Mordecai Manuel Noah (1785-1851). Noah was the grandson of community leader Jonas Phillips (mentioned earlier). In his own time, Noah was perhaps most famous as a popular playwright, the Neil Simon of his day – with one difference: Noah had little talent, and his plays are forgotten today.

Noah viewed politics as his real calling. He edited a Democratic newspaper, got elected Grand Sachem (that is, Grand "Macher") of Tammany Hall, and was named consul to Tunis by President Madison. Shortly after taking up his post, Noah was fired by Secretary of State

James Monroe. Monroe's reason was religious. He stated bluntly that had he known that Noah was Jewish, he wouldn't have appointed him to a post in Tunis. Noah was furious, and rallied his friends (who would have written angry op-ed articles in the New York Times, had there been a New York Times back then), but the decision stood.

Noah bounced back with other local political appointments: Surveyor of the Port of New York (whatever that was) and Sheriff of New York. He was also involved in community activities as a leader of Shearith Israel.

Today, Noah is best known for his Ararat project: His grand scheme to build a Jewish homeland on Grand Island near Buffalo. In formulating this plan, Noah may have been influenced by the thinking of Gershom Seixas. In 1798, President John "Not Quincy" Adams almost led the United States into a war with France over something called the XYZ Affair involving French rudeness. (I'm not kidding; you can look it up.) Adams declared May 9th a day of prayer, to support the government, pray for peace, etc.

Many of the sermons delivered on this day of prayer were the usual tripe, but Seixas, for some reason, spoke about something different. He said that the United States was the best place in the history of the world for Jews to live. However, despite that, Jews should never forget their one true homeland: Palestine.[1]

Noah felt the same way. He believed that Palestine should become the Jewish homeland. His writings on the subject show that he had a great awareness of the big power interests that would have to be balanced to achieve that dream. Unfortunately for Noah, not only were his Herzl-like ideas ahead of their time, but the United States was a backwater of world Jewry, further reducing his influence.

In any event, Noah believed that until Palestine could become the Jewish state, there had to be some place where Jews could find refuge in a land of their own. He chose Grand Island between the U.S. and Canada

---

1. Seixas didn't ignore the France issue. Rather than delivering an anti-French sermon, as the Federalists wanted all ministers to do, Seixas spoke favorably of the help France had given the U.S. in the Revolution 20 years earlier.

near Buffalo. Noah, dressed like the High Priest in Raiders of the Lost Ark, conducted an elaborate opening ceremony, after which the Ararat plan went nowhere. Why not? Have you ever been to Buffalo in the winter? There were no customers for Ararat, and all that's left today of the scheme is a plaque on the site.[1]

As with his other defeats, Noah rebounded to continue his writing and politicking. He was a shameless self-promoter, and in that respect, is much more a man of the late 20th century than of the early 19th.

Uriah Phillips Levy

Uriah P. Levy (1792-1862) was another grandson of Jonas Phillips, and thus, Noah's cousin. When he was ten, Levy did something most un-Jewish: He ran away to sea. He spent much of the War of 1812 as a POW of the British. Afterwards, he slowly rose through the ranks. But Levy had one little problem: A monstrous temper that was set off by even a hint of anti-Semitism – and the Navy had plenty of that in those days. He was always getting into fights or duels with other officers over perceived anti-Semitic slights. The hostility to Levy only increased when he successfully eliminated the practice of flogging from the Navy, thus thwarting many American Captain Blighs.

As a result of all his fights, Levy was court-martialed six times, and emerged with a perfect batting average: He was found guilty each time. Levy went years without a sea command, but he refused to resign. Finally, in 1855, he was dismissed as part of a general layoff of naval personnel (sort of an 1850s peace dividend). He refused to leave, and demanded to appear before a Naval Court of Inquiry.

Amazingly, in 1858, he finally won a case (probably because he finally hired a good lawyer), and was reinstated. In 1859, he was given his first command in 15 years. The following year, he was named commander of

---

1. Noah should have established Ararat in those islands where there were already Jewish settlements, like Curacao or Barbados. He might have had better luck.

the entire Mediterranean squadron.[1] Levy used his proximity to Palestine to bring thousands of pounds of dirt from the Holy Land aboard his warship to be used by American Jews who wanted to be buried in sacred soil. He retired soon thereafter, with the title Commodore Levy. As another sign that the Navy recognized his attributes, Levy had a destroyer named for him in World War II.

Levy made a significant contribution to the preservation of American history. He was long an admirer of Thomas Jefferson. After the former president died in 1826, his home, Monticello, started falling to pieces. Levy bought it, restored it, and kept it up. After Levy's death, Monticello was given to his nephew, Jefferson Levy (what a perfect name!), who sold it to the U.S. government in whose hands it has remained ever since.[2]

Levy's image in history is that of a proud Jew fighting anti-Semitism. However, his kid brother was also a naval officer, but, as far as we can tell, never had a single fight over anti-Semitism. Either Levy's temper led him to see anti-Semitism where it didn't exist; or naval officers didn't want to mess with the younger Levy because they didn't want to start a fight with the older brother; or the younger brother was a wimp. We don't know which explanation is correct.

Isaac Leeser

Isaac Leeser (1806-1868) was the leading American Jewish religious leader in the pre-Civil War era, until eclipsed by his rival, Isaac Mayer Wise. He came to the United States in 1824, and worked as a clerk in his uncle's store in Richmond. More knowledgeable about Judaism than most other immigrants, Leeser assisted Hazzan Isaac Seixas[3] of the Richmond synagogue. He also wrote a series of articles in the local paper, the

---

1. Sure, it sounds impressive. But how many ships could the tiny American Navy have had in the Mediterranean in 1860?
2. No, he didn't make money on the deal; he sold it for cost.
3. Do you get the feeling that if your name was "Isaac," you were fated to have a career in religion?

Richmond Whig, defending Judaism. This brought him to the attention of Philadelphia's Mikveh Israel, which hired him as its hazzan in 1829, when Leeser was only 23.

The only major change Leeser made in the service was his introduction of an English Sabbath sermon. Based on the quality of many rabbis' Sabbath sermons in today's America, it may not be a contribution of which he would be proud.

Today, Leeser is claimed as an ancestor by both Orthodoxy and Conservatism. In his own beliefs, Leeser would best be characterized as Modern Orthodox. He never called himself "rabbi," as many other non-ordained religious leaders did (including Wise), because he was too modest to assume a title he didn't possess. In 1850, he had a disagreement with the Mikveh Israel board, and left (or was pushed). However, as so often happens in the United States, an ousted rabbi has followers who will set up another synagogue for him. That happened to Leeser, who remained hazzan of his own synagogue until his death.

Leeser was a prolific writer. He published the first English translation of the Jewish Bible in 1854, which remained the standard work until surpassed by a new translation in 1917. Leeser also published instruction books about Judaism for children. In pre-Civil War America, Leeser was probably best known for his newspaper, The Occident. That paper was published from April, 1843 until 1869, and was the first regularly-appearing Jewish newspaper in the United States. In it, Leeser reprinted sermons and reported on Jewish communities throughout the nation and the world. The only things missing from The Occident were large ads from Jewish organizations plugging their upcoming testimonial dinners. Despite that gap, Leeser's paper remains an important source of 19th century Jewish history.

Leeser's main goal in life was a unified American Jewish community. To achieve that, he was even willing to participate in the 1855 Cleveland Conference of Jewish religious leaders, despite the fact that the conference would be dominated by Reformers. Nothing, however, was accomplished in Cleveland (as we shall see later).

In 1867, he finally realized another dream, the opening of Maimonides College, the first American institution for training rabbis. Maimonides didn't survive Leeser's death, and closed down soon thereafter with only three students.

Among the major leaders of American Jewish history, Leeser stands as one of the giants. Unfortunately for him, he was fated to live in the wrong era. Reform was taking over, and by the time of Leeser's death, there were few traditional synagogues left in America.[1] His contribution was to keep the fires of traditionalism burning so there would be something left to revive when the East European Jews arrived after 1881.

Leeser was lonely personally as well as professionally. He never married. Some say it was because he was, to be quite blunt, an ugly duckling (due to a bout with smallpox). However, men uglier than Leeser get married every day. Perhaps the real reason lay in demographics. Leeser, bright and demanding, could not find the right girl in the relatively small pool of available women.[2] In any event, he devoted his total energies on behalf of the community, and deserves greater recognition than he gets today.

Two Political Crises

Two crises before the Civil War brought the American Jewish community closer than it had been earlier. The first was the Damascus Blood Libel Affair of 1840. The head of the Franciscan monastery in Damascus disappeared. Rumors spread that the Jews had killed the priest to use his blood for either a) wine; b) matzos; or c) both. Thirteen Jews were arrested.

---

1. That's why Leeser came in second place to Wise in a recent poll of American Jewish historians on the question: Who was the greatest American Jewish leader of the nineteenth century?

2. The perfect woman for him would have been Rebecca Gratz, his partner in Jewish educational efforts. Gratz, pretty and intelligent, was Sir Walter Scott's model for the Rebecca in Ivanhoe. Just one problem: Gratz was 25 years older than Leeser, proving, once again, that in life, timing is everything.

Under torture, they confessed to the charges. In the midst of this affair, the French consul and Catholic priests throughout Europe spread the blood libel charge far and wide.

Eventually, Moses Montefiore and Adolphe Cremieux, the leaders of British and French Jewry respectively, interceded with Egypt's Mehmet Ali, the ruler of Damascus. They politely informed Ali that a British gunboat near Cairo was ready to start using Ali's palace for target practice. In a flash, Ali ordered the surviving Jews freed.[1]

The U.S., as stated earlier, was a backwater of world Jewry. But that didn't prevent American Jews from organizing protests of the Damascus Affair. First they held rallies in major cities. Next, representatives came together to ask President Martin Van Buren to do something to aid their Syrian brethren. This marks the first time that joint action, as Jews for a Jewish cause, was undertaken by the community.[2]

Van Buren heeded the Jews' appeal (perhaps because he was a New York Democrat and Tammany Hall leader), and instructed Secretary of State Forsyth to express American displeasure over the Damascus situation. Mehmet Ali couldn't have cared less about American displeasure; the U.S. had no gunboats in Cairo harbor. Nevertheless, American Jews were gratified over what they had accomplished: They had successfully organized and petitioned the president over a matter of concern to them.

Isaac Leeser hoped that community leaders would now see the importance of unity. He tried to use this success as a stepping stone to organize American Jewry on a permanent basis by establishing some sort of national Jewish council. His plan went nowhere. Leeser suspected sabotage on the part of Shearith Israel, which, he thought, did not want to give up its honor as the "mother synagogue" to a national organization.

---

1. Essay question: Using the example just given, explain how wimpy American responses to radical provocations in the Middle East have led to terrorists' stepping all over the United States.
2. In other words, this was the ancestor of Save Soviet Jewry rallies.

To anyone who knows anything about the American Jewish community, none of this should be surprising.

A result of the Damascus Affair was a further confirmation of the negative view Jews had towards the Catholic Church. These feelings intensified during the second crisis, the Mortara Affair.

In 1858, papal police in Bologna, Italy, kidnapped a six-year-old Jewish boy named Edgar Mortara from his home. When his parents tried to retrieve him, they were rebuffed. The Pope's people said that when Edgar was one-year-old, he had gotten sick. His worried nurse had him baptized as a Catholic so that he wouldn't die as a (gasp!) Jew. Therefore, Edgar is now a Catholic, and the Church can keep him.

Naturally, the Mortaras were horrified, as was most of the world. Nations and individuals not known for friendliness to Jews all condemned the Vatican's actions. Despite the outcry, Pope Pius IX refused to give Edgar up.

In the U.S., Jews rallied as they had 18 years earlier, but this time, the president refused to help. James Buchanan was an old unmarried fool (Yiddish: "alter kocker") who spent most of his time failing to prevent the Civil War. As a former Secretary of State, he was not sympathetic to Jewish interests. More importantly, Buchanan did not want to alienate Irish Catholic voters who made up much of the Democratic Party.

This failure finally caused the Jewish community to establish a national organization to protect its interests. It was called the Board of Delegates of American Israelites,[1] and consisted of representatives of synagogues from throughout the country. The Board served as the Jewish voice when problems arose during the Civil War, as we will see in the next chapter. Eventually, the Board was absorbed by the Union of American Hebrew Congregations.

And what happened to poor little Edgar? He was never returned to his parents. In 1870, when the Vatican lost its secular powers, the 18-year-old

---

1. In those days, Jews hated calling anything "Jewish." They preferred "Hebrew" or "Israelite."

Edgar was free, but it was too late; he'd already been brainwashed, and was well on his way to becoming a priest. He lived a long, Catholic life, dying in Belgium in 1940. The irony is that had he lived only a few months longer, Edgar, who had never known what it was to live as a Jew, would have learned what it was to die as a Jew.

The Mortara and Damascus Affairs led many Jews to sympathize with anti-Catholic nativist groups such as the Know-Nothing Party. The Know-Nothings were not anti-Semitic – in fact, one of the few Know-Nothing congressmen was a Jew named Levin – rather, they focused their attacks on Catholics. In the mid-1800s, to Jews, Catholicism represented anti-Semitism. Many of them had immigrated from Catholic southern Germany, where their lives had been unpleasant, to say the least. Some Jews felt that the enemy of my enemy is my friend, and thus supported the Know-Nothings.[1]

Not surprisingly, the Mortara Affair further exacerbated Jewish anti-Catholic opinions. In fact, these feelings were not reduced until the immigration of the Eastern European Jews. On the Lower East Side, they lived near and worked with Italian immigrants. Through the years, Jews and Italians developed closer relations than Jews had had with other Catholic groups. Eventually, Jews came to distinguish between the different Catholic ethnic groups, the Vatican, and the local church, and assess each group individually.

Religion in Pre-War America, or Reform, the Wave of the Future

As the nineteenth century arrived, the Sephardic ritual started losing its monopoly in the United States. The first break came in Philadelphia in 1802, with the founding of Rodeph Shalom, America's first Ashkenazic synagogue. The real nail in the coffin of Sephardi domination came in

---

1. The Know-Nothings' main problem was their name. Admit it. Wouldn't you feel just a little bit stupid voting for a party called "Know-Nothing?"

1825, when some members of Shearith Israel broke away to form Bnai Jeshurun, New York's first Ashkenazic congregation.

Other pre-War religious developments on the traditional front included the 1840 arrival of Abraham Rice, the first ordained rabbi in America. Rice led a congregation in Baltimore, and was miserable the rest of his life. Religious observance in America was minimal, and there was nothing Rice could do about it. He died broken-hearted in 1862, still angry at himself for not having bought a round-trip ticket 22 years earlier.

In 1849, a different sort of Orthodox rabbi arrived. Bernard Illowy had been a participant in the 1848 democratic revolution in Austria-Hungary, and was forced to flee after its collapse. He was also the first American rabbi with a doctorate. Due to his worldly experience, Illowy was never as down-hearted about American Jewry as Rice was. He simply tried to do his best in a land of little belief.

In 1852, the first Eastern European synagogue ("shul") was founded in New York. Beis Hamedrash Hagadol, led by Rabbi Abraham Joseph Asch, was the precursor to the hundreds of Orthodox shuls that would be established in America with the mass immigration of the Russian Jews in 1881.

Soon after it was founded, Beis Hamedrash Hagadol became a tiny minority among American synagogues: A traditional speck in a sea of Reform. Reform Judaism had begun in Germany in 1810. The first stirrings in the U.S. occurred in 1824 in Charleston's venerable Beth Elohim congregation. A young playwright named Isaac Harby led a group that seceded from the old synagogue after it refused to make changes in the service. (Maybe this is where South Carolina get the idea for secession from the Union.) Harby moved to New York and the effort collapsed. By 1836, however, the Reformers were in the majority, and they took over Beth Elohim. It was the traditionalists who were forced to start a new synagogue.

Another milestone for Reform was the establishment of Baltimore's Har Sinai, the first Reform temple established as such. Reform called for changes in the liturgy, shortening it and putting in more English. It also called for the use of an organ.[1]

The stage was set for the rise of **The** Reform leader, Isaac Mayer Wise (1819-1900). Wise arrived in the U.S. in 1844, and soon obtained a pulpit in Albany, New York. He started with his moderate reforms there, but some congregants disagreed with him, leading to a fistfight between Wise and a congregant.[2]

Wise left for the greener pastures of Cincinnati, where he stayed for 50 years, making that city the center for Reform Judaism until today. Rabbi Dr. Wise was neither a rabbi nor a doctor, but was the most important Jewish leader of the 19th century.[3]

Wise was a deeply patriotic American and a proud Jew. He saw the synagogue as an Americanizing influence that had to be reformed to reflect that aspect. Thus, he established a new liturgy, "Minhag America:" No references to either sacrifices, resurrection, or Zion.[4]

Like his rival, Leeser, Wise's main goal was a unified American Jewry. To achieve that, he went to the Cleveland Conference (mentioned earlier in connection with Leeser). Wise made concessions to traditional beliefs, and accepted the authority of the Talmud as the source of Jewish law. But that led to bitter attacks on Wise by the Eastern Reformers led by Baltimore's Radical Reformer David Einhorn. The Conference fell apart under the pressure. Unlike the strident ideologue Einhorn, Wise was focused on his goal of unity. He would prefer that it be achieved through moderation, but if radical Reform would lead to unity, he'd be for that instead (as we'll see later on).

---

1. The organ issue shows Reform's rejection of its roots. A truly Jewish-minded Reform group would use a Jewish instrument during the services, namely, a violin.
2. That's the problem with American Judaism today: Rabbis never get into fistfights with their congregants anymore. Think of the possibilities: The sisterhood could sell tickets and turn it into a fundraiser.
3. At least, he was voted that title by a panel of historians a few years ago, and I see no reason to disagree.
4. The Reform attitude was America is our Zion, and Cincinnati is our Jerusalem.

Among Orthodox Jews, Wise is the villain, the man who almost single-handedly pulled America into the Reform camp. Despite having learned that in my younger days in Orthodox day school, I like Wise a lot more than I used to. Sure, he had faults: He was arrogant (a typically German trait), insulting, and weak-willed during the 1885 Pittsburgh Conference. On the other hand, he was a forceful leader whose organizational skills not only led to a unified Reform movement, but provided the impetus (as we'll see, in a negative reaction) for unified Orthodox and Conservative movements.

The swift manner in which he took offense at any perceived anti-Semitism would have made Commodore Levy proud. Unlike many later Reform rabbis, Wise's vision of social justice put Jews first, the rest of the world a distant second.

Reform, especially in Wise's eyes, was never meant as a rejection of Judaism. Rather, it was a method of combining Judaism with Americanism. Had the Reformers merely wanted to ape Protestantism, they would have never built temples in the exotic Moorish style, so unlike the architecture of any American church. In addition, early Reform Jews did not necessarily give up their religious practices. Many Jewish businessmen kept their stores closed on Saturdays. Others observed the Sabbath in some fashion. In more rural and pioneering areas, Jews showed their commitment to their religion by circumcising their sons. Mohelim (ritual circumcisers) traveled hundreds of miles throughout the American West performing "brisses."

Synagogues themselves were becoming less relevant to the lives of American Jews. In 1843, a group of young men founded a secular Jewish organization called "B'nai B'rith" (Sons of the Covenant). B'nai B'rith combined Jewishness with the American tradition of joining groups. B'nai B'rith grew quickly, and 150 years later, is still an important organization in the community, especially its youth group. B'nai B'rith served another function in the 1800s: It was neutral turf where Reformers and Traditionalists could get together as Jews.

Chicago: Its Origins

The first half of the 19th century saw the establishment of many Jewish communities throughout the Midwest. Chicago serves as a paradigm of these communities, because it is the biggest and because it is the city where this book was written.

The first Jews settled in Chicago in 1841. By 1845, there were enough men for a minyan for Yom Kippur services. Abraham Kohn[1] provided the Torah scroll. The service was delayed many times because they had exactly ten men, and were missing a "pisherman" (the eleventh man whose presence allows the service to continue while one of the congregants goes to the bathroom).

Abraham Kohn's mother, Dilah, lived with him. She was a frail woman who would eat no meat not properly slaughtered according to Jewish law (i.e., "schechted"). She was living on bread and potatoes and complained to Abraham, "Abe, darling, I'd give anything for some chicken soup or a hamburger." The Jewish community was growing, so Kohn decided to kill two birds with one stone. He hired Ignatz Kunreuther[2] as the community's first schochet and rabbi (Kunreuther was very knowledgeable, but not ordained).

With the rabbi hired, the synagogue was officially established on November 3, 1847 under the name Kehilat Anshe Maarav, Congregation of the Men of the West. As the years went by, "Maarav" was spelled various ways, usually "Mayriv." Thus, "Congregation of the Men of the West" became pronounced as "Congregation of the Men of the Night." That implied that the synagogue was for either workers on the graveyard shift or vampires. The congregation resolved the problem by simply using initials, and today the synagogue is known as KAM.

Not everyone felt wanted at KAM. The synagogue was run by Bavarian Jews, and "Polish" Jews (actually, from Posen) felt left out. What do Jews

---

1. Remember him? He's the peddler who tried to sell to the messianic sect.
2. A mouthful of a name. Interestingly, his great-great-granddaughter is a leading member of the Chicago Jewish Historical Society.

who feel uncomfortable in their synagogue do? Leave, of course, and make a new one, which is just what the Polish Jews did.[1]

So by 1852, Chicago had two synagogues, both traditional. But, as elsewhere in America, the wave of Reform was sweeping over Chicago. KAM started taking tentative steps in the direction of moderate Reform. That was too much for Kunreuther, who resigned rather than be part of changes he didn't believe in. By 1857, KAM was divided between the moderate Reformers led by Abraham Kohn and the radical Reformers led by Chicago's first Jewish alderman, Henry Greenebaum.

The radicals won out, but voluntarily left anyway. Rather than split KAM, they established their own temple, one that would be Reform from the beginning. It was called Temple Sinai, and to this day remains an exponent of radical Reform. As in other midwestern cities, virtually all the synagogues founded in the Civil War era were established by German Jews, began Orthodox and shifted to Reform (including the Polish synagogue).

---

1. An irony of history: Through a series of mergers, too long and complicated to discuss here, the breakaway Polish synagogue merged back into KAM about 30 years ago.

CHAPTER 3

THE CIVIL WAR

Jews and Slavery – Why There Were No Slaves Named Goldberg[1]

In the mid-1800s, slavery was America's great moral issue. Debate was filled with violence, invective, self-righteousness, and Bible-thumping; in short, slavery was the abortion issue of the 1800s.

The anti-slavery movement was personified by the Abolitionists. One of the best-known Jewish Abolitionists was August Bondi, who rode with John Brown. Unlike Brown, who fulfilled his desire to become a martyr by being hanged in 1859, Bondi had a stronger survival instinct: He died in bed in 1907.

Bondi, however, was an exception. Most Jews were anti-slavery, but not card-carrying Abolitionists. Why not? One reason was that the Abolitionists were filled with the spirit of religious Christian moralism – a big turn-off to potential Jewish members.

Another reason was the double standard of the Abolitionist leaders. They would say to the Jews: "You, of all people, should join us. After all,

---

1. C'mon, now. You don't really think Whoopi Goldberg is her real name? Incidentally, do you know Whoopi's real name? The answer is at the end of this chapter.

weren't you slaves in Egypt?" When Jews expressed reluctance to join up, many Abolitionists turned on them fiercely. Isaac Mayer Wise denounced this double standard, and considered the Abolitionists a bunch of anti-Semitic hypocrites.[1]

The Abolitionists would be proud that their liberal Protestant double standard regarding Jews still exists in today's America as a double standard against Israel. In fact, the National Council of Churches combines liberal Christianity with anti-Israel sentiments, making it a true descendant of the Abolitionists.

Despite their problems with the Abolitionists, only a few Jews, some of those in the South, favored slavery. Not many Jews owned plantations, where slaves were needed in great numbers. It's hard to imagine a Jew sitting on a verandah, sipping a mint julep, ordering Simon Legree to whip some slaves. A real Jew would give his slaves breaks during the day for coffee and cake. Maybe that's what southern Jews actually did. Even in the South, Jews were primarily store owners. Only 1/4 of southern Jews owned slaves, usually only one or two. These servants were less like plantation slaves and more like live-in help. The only differences were that slaves understood English and didn't get paid in cash.

Back in the North, Jews got ensnared in the slavery debate on the eve of the Civil War. Morris J. Raphall was the well-known rabbi of New York's Bnai Jeshurun. In 1860, he became the first Jewish clergyman to open a session of Congress with a prayer. On January 4, 1861, Raphall stated in a sermon that despite Abolitionist claims to the contrary, nothing in the Bible forbade slavery. In fact, the black slaves were descendants of Noah's son, Ham, and were thus destined to be enslaved. However, owners were obligated to treat their slaves kindly.

The sermon ignited a firestorm of protest in the North. Raphall's position was attacked by all anti-slavery Jewish leaders from the traditional/Orthodox (Sabato Morais) to radical Reform (David Einhorn).

---

1. Whoa! What about Reform Judaism's belief in social justice? Remember the last chapter: Wise believed in Jews first, the rest of the world second.

Even supporters of Raphall's position, like Wise, thought the Ham reference was going too far.

In the South, the reaction was different. Copies of Raphall's sermon were distributed as proof of Biblical approval of slavery. Not surprisingly, the part about treating slaves kindly was overlooked.

Poor Raphall: Attacked as pro-slavery, he was really a strong Union backer. His son, Alfred, lost an arm at Gettysburg. All Raphall thought he was doing was delivering a sermon on the Bible, ignoring the political realities. His true crime was naiveté.

The Civil War: General Salomon and General Grant

There were about 7,000 Jews in the Union Army; 2,000 in the Confederate. This is a conservative estimate. Historian Henry Feingold thinks the total number in both armies was 10,000.

Author Gore Vidal, in his anti-Semitic kvetch to Norman Podhoretz some years back, complained that Jews didn't care about the Civil War, implying that the reason was that Jews played no part in the conflict. However, over 6% of the American Jewish population of 150,000 served in the two armies (the equivalent of more than 300,000 Jewish soldiers today). That's about the same percentage as the general population. Also, Jews, who made up only 1/2 of 1% of the population, made up a similar percentage of the armies. So Gore, take these numbers and...you get my drift.[1]

The most famous Jewish participant in the Civil War was Judah P. Benjamin. This former Louisiana senator served as Confederate Attorney-General, Secretary of War, and Secretary of State. Benjamin, as might be expected of a plantation-owning slaveholder, had **NO** Jewish identity. He

---

1.   Vidal isn't alone in his attitude that Jews had no part in the Civil War. In an October, 1994, Forbes magazine story about Disney's lost fight to build a theme park near the sight of the Battle of Bull Run in Virginia, actor Robert Duvall said, "It's like building at Auschwitz. But then [Disney head Michael] Eisner's ancestors only came over in the last 100 years. The Civil War isn't part of his history."

was married to a Catholic girl, and never participated in any Jewish activities.

Naturally, this didn't stop his enemies from yelling "Jew, Jew." Many Northerners cursed the Jew Benjamin as a Judas who betrayed the Union (having a first name like Judah made that connection easy). Many Southerners blamed Benjamin for their losses; he obviously was slacking off on the job, or worse, profiting from it. After the War, Benjamin fled to England, became a British attorney, wrote a leading textbook on sales law, and died as a prominent British subject.

The heart of Jewish pro-Union sentiment was in Illinois, the Land of Lincoln, specifically, Chicago, and its 1000-1500 Jews. After the War began, even the Democratic Stephen Douglas fans switched enthusiastically to Lincoln. When Honest Abe left for Washington, Abraham Kohn, now Chicago City Clerk, on behalf of the Jewish community, presented the president-elect with a specially-made American flag. Along the white stripes, in Hebrew, were verses from the Book of Joshua encouraging the Israelites to "be strong and of good courage."

In August, 1862, Lincoln issued one of his periodic calls for troops. The Chicago Jewish community gathered in a mass meeting, determined to raise $10,000 to equip a 100-man Jewish company.[1] In only three days, the community raised $11,000 as well as the manpower for the company (which became Company C of the 82nd Illinois Regiment). In the end, 8-10% of Chicago's Jewish population fought in the War, a huge percentage.

One of those Jews was Edward S. Salomon, a man whose rapid rise in American life was remarkable even by 19th century standards. He arrived in Chicago in 1855, an 18-year-old immigrant from northern Germany. He worked in a cap store, studied law, and was admitted to the Illinois Bar in 1859. Politically ambitious, Salomon was elected 6th Ward Alderman a year later.

---

1. Now that's a great way to keep down a war-time deficit: Get volunteers to pay their own way.

In 1861, Lincoln issued a call for troops (this is a year before the other call for troops, but bear with me; I'll get back to it). Salomon volunteered, and was named second lieutenant in the 24th Illinois Regiment, under Colonel Frederick Hecker. Hecker, a non-Jew, had fought for Jewish rights in Germany in the 1840s. He was admired by the Jews of Chicago, most of whom had emigrated from Germany.

The 24th, however, was not called into action. Despite that, Salomon kept receiving promotions: To captain, and then to major, all while serving in the Chicago City Council and practicing law.[1] In August, 1862, the 82nd Illinois regiment was formed, with Hecker named as its commander. Salomon was named second-in-command, with yet another promotion, to lieutenant-colonel. The 82nd included the Jewish Company C (I told you I'd get back to it).

After receiving all these easy promotions, Salomon finally had to get to work: The 82nd was ordered into action and Salomon resigned from the City Council. The Regiment's first battle was Chancellorsville, but Salomon did not participate: He got sick and was recuperating back in Chicago. That's one of the good things about a civil war: If you get sick, your own bed isn't too far away.

The next battle was Gettysburg, in July, 1863. Salomon commanded the Regiment, because Hecker had been injured at Chancellorsville. Gettysburg was to be Salomon's big moment. The Rebels had captured Union rifle pits, and the 82nd was ordered to take them back. Salomon, on horseback, led the charge. His horse was shot dead from under him. Salomon fell, bruised and injured. Ignoring his condition, Salomon got on another horse, and again led the charge. Again, his horse was shot dead from under him, throwing him hard to the ground. Salomon looked for a third horse, but could find no volunteers, the horses viewing him as bad luck. So he led the charge on foot. This time, the 82nd was successful, and captured the rifle pits.

---

1. If officers could be promoted that way today, the army would see many more volunteers, at least among aldermen and lawyers.

Salomon's actions received much praise from his commanding officers. General O.O. Howard (as in Howard University) sent Salomon to take charge of a mutinous Pennsylvania regiment. Salomon whipped them in to shape (not literally; remember, Uriah Levy had gotten rid of that practice). General Howard then had Salomon attached to his staff for a while, before Salomon finally got permission to return to the 82nd, along with a promotion to full colonel.

In 1864, Hecker resigned from the Army, and Salomon became commander of the 82nd. Thus, it was Salomon who led the Regiment back to Chicago in triumph in June, 1865. He had been named a brevet brigadier-general. "Brevet" was quasi-honorary; it meant that if Salomon stayed in the Army, his rank would be kicked down to colonel. Salomon, however, left the Army after the War, so he remained "General" Salomon the rest of his life.

In America, the tradition was for war heroes to run for office (now war heroes go on the lecture circuit for big bucks). Salomon was no exception. In November, 1865, he easily won election as a Republican for Cook County Clerk. Salomon was only 28 years old; he had been in America for only 10 years.

Four years later, President Grant named Salomon governor of Washington Territory. He also served as honorary head of the seven-person Jewish community of Olympia, the territorial capital, and led Yom Kippur services there. On the whole, Salomon was a good governor. Unfortunately, he also got caught up in the loose morals of the times: He took money from the territorial treasury to use for a personal investment. The matter became public, and Salomon reimbursed the Territory in full, but he was forced to resign after only two years in office.

Salomon moved to San Francisco, where he practiced law, participated in politics, and become California commander of the Grand Army of the Republic (the Union veterans group). His last public appearance was to deliver a speech in July, 1913, commemorating the 50th anniversary of the Battle of Gettysburg. He died a few weeks later, survived by a daughter and his son, the doctor (and not just a doctor, a specialist, a gastroenterologist).

Other Jews also rose to high ranks in the Army, the highest being Major-General Frederick Knefler. Marcus Spiegel (as in Chicago-based Spiegel catalogue fame) was slated for promotion to general (not brevet, but for real), when he was killed in action in 1864. On the Confederate side, David Camden de Leon served as the Surgeon-General (I suppose that's a more typically "Jewish" task).

The Jewish soldiers in the Civil War were not religious, but they tried to celebrate the important holidays as best they could. One of the most fascinating accounts of a Passover seder comes out of the Civil War. The account, which is both hysterically funny and deeply moving, was written by Joseph Joel in the Jewish Messenger in 1866, and is reprinted in its entirety:

"In the commencement of the war in 1861, I enlisted from Cleveland, Ohio, in the Union cause and became attached to the 23rd Regiment, one of the first sent from the Buckeye State.

"Our destination was West Virginia. We encountered on the 10th of September, 1861, at Carnifax Ferry, the forces under the rebel General Floyd and were ordered to take up our position at the foot of Sewen Mountain. We remained there until we marched to the village of Fayette, to take it and establish there our winter quarters, having again routed General Floyd and his forces.

"While lying there our camp duties were not of an arduous character, and being apprised of the approaching Festival of Passover, twenty of my comrades and co-religionists belonging to the Regiment, united in a request to our commanding officer for relief from duty, in order that we might keep the holy days, which he readily acceded to.

"The first point was gained and, as the Paymaster had lately visited the Regiment, he had left us plenty of greenbacks. Our next business was to find some suitable person to proceed to Cincinnati, Ohio, to buy us matzos. Our sutler [a private person who supplies food and other material to the army], being a co-religionist, and going home to that city, readily undertook to send them.

"We were anxiously awaiting to receive our matzos, and about the middle of the morning of Erev Pesach a supply train arrived in camp, and to our delight seven barrels of matzos. On opening them we were surprised and pleased to find that our thoughtful sutler had enclosed two Hagodahs and prayer books. We were now able to keep the Seder nights, if we could only obtain the other requisites for that occasion. We had a consultation and decided to send parties to forage in the country while a party stayed to build a log hut for the services.[1] About the middle of the afternoon, the foragers arrived, having been quite successful. We obtained two kegs of cider, a lamb, several chickens, and some eggs. Horseradish or parsley we could not obtain, but in lieu we found a weed, whose bitterness, I apprehended, exceeded anything our forefathers 'enjoyed.'

"We were still in a great quandary. We had the lamb, but did not know what part was to represent it at the table; but Yankee ingenuity prevailed, and it was decided to cook the whole and put it on the table, then we could dine off it, and be sure we got the right part. The necessaries for the charoses we could not obtain, so we got a brick which, rather hard to digest, reminded us, by looking at it, for what purposes it was intended.[2]

"At dark we had all prepared, and were ready to commence the service. There being no chazan present, I was selected to read the services, which I commenced by asking the blessing of the Almighty on the food before us, and to preserve our lives from danger. The ceremonies were passing off very nicely, until we arrived at the part where the bitter herb was to be taken. We all had a large portion of the herb ready to eat at the moment I said the blessing; each eats his portion when, horrors! what a scene ensued in our little congregation, it is impossible for my pen to describe. The herb was very bitter and very fiery like Cayenne pepper, and excited our thirst to such a degree, that we forgot the law authorizing us to drink

---

1. Obviously, this regiment was equally prepared for the holiday of Succot.
2. Since charoses symbolizes the Israelites' making of bricks in Egypt, Joel's use of a brick here is quite clever.

only four cups, and the consequence was that we drank up all the cider. Those that drank more freely, became excited, and one thought he was Moses, another Aaron, and one had the audacity to call himself a Pharaoh. The consequence was a skirmish, with no one hurt, only Moses, Aaron, and Pharaoh had to be carried away to the camp, and there left in the arms of Morpheus. This slight incident did not take away our appetite, and, after doing justice to the lamb, chickens and eggs, we resumed the second portion of the service without anything occurring worthy of note.

"There, in the wild woods of West Virginia, away from home and friends, we consecrated and offered up to the ever-loving God of Israel our prayers and sacrifice. I doubt whether the spirits of our forefathers, had they been looking down on us, standing there with our arms by our sides ready for an attack, faithful to our God and our cause, would have imagined themselves among mortals, enacting this commemoration of the scene that transpired in Egypt.

"Since then a number of my comrades have fallen in battle in defending the flag they volunteered to protect with their lives. I have myself received a number of wounds, all but mortal, but there is no occasion in my life that gives me more pleasure and satisfaction than when I remember the celebration of Passover of 1862."

The desire to practice their religion led to one of the two Jewish controversies of the Civil War: The chaplaincy matter. According to federal law, a chaplain had to be "a regular ordained minister of some Christian denomination." Guess who that leaves out. Interestingly, the Confederacy had no such restriction; but it had no Jewish chaplains either.

A Jew named Michael Allen was serving as a lay chaplain for a heavily Jewish Pennsylvania regiment, led by Colonel Max Friedman. Allen was discovered by a YMCA worker. In those days, the YMCA put its main emphasis on the "C," and the worker complained about Allen's presence, getting him fired. The regiment's Jews challenged the law by having Rev. Arnold Fischel, a teacher at Shearith Israel, apply to be their chaplain. Friedman's commander reluctantly turned down the request, saying he was bound by the law.

The Board of Delegates of American Israelites lobbied to get the law changed. In December, 1861, Lincoln promised to remove the "Christian" restriction. It took another seven months to actually amend the statute, to allow for Jewish chaplains. Why so long? Hey, there's a war on, for Pete's sake; we can't get to everything right away.

The second controversy was more serious. The border between Union and Confederate lines was fluid, changing with each battle. The border areas became a smuggler's paradise. The northern manufacturers needed southern cotton for their factories; the South needed northern gold to pay for basic goods from Europe. Smugglers served as the means of exchange.

The Union, trying to starve the South into surrender, wanted to stop the smuggling. That proved to be impossible; too many Union Army officers were making too much money from the illegal activity. Among the civilians involved were Jews. As with most endeavors, Jews excelled in this activity.

In December, 1862, in response to the smuggling, General Ulysses S. Grant issued the infamous Order No. 11:

"The Jews, as a class violating every regulation of trade established by the Treasury Department and also department orders, are hereby expelled from the department within 24 hours from the receipt of this Order.

"Post commanders will see that all of this class of people be furnished passes and required to leave, and any one returning after such notification will be arrested and held in confinement until an opportunity occurs of sending them out as prisoners, unless furnished with permit from headquarters.

"No passes will be given these people to visit headquarters for the purpose of making personal application for trade permits.

"By order of Maj. Gen. U.S. Grant."

Hold on, Grant! Why are you picking on us? We were just a small part of the overall smuggling activity. Arthur Hertzberg, in his history of American Jews, disagrees. He implies that Grant was right to single out Jews, since we were such a major part of the smuggling activity. Puh-leez,

Rabbi Dr. Hertzberg. The "blame the victim" rationale for anti-Semitism is passé.

In any event, the Jews were ordered out of Grant's area: Parts of western Kentucky, western Tennessee, and northern Mississippi. Cesar Kaskel, a Jewish community leader from Paducah, Kentucky, ran to Washington to let Lincoln know about Order No. 11. Kaskel was joined by other leaders from the Board of Delegates in presenting his case. Lincoln told them not to worry, that he would immediately direct Grant to revoke the Order. Had there been phones then, Lincoln probably would have screamed at Grant and accused him of sleeping through his U.S. Constitution class at West Point. But in 1862, news traveled more slowly; before the Order was revoked, some Jewish communities were actually expelled.

For over a century, historians have debated why Grant would issue such an anti-Semitic unconstitutional Order. In the history of the United States, Order No. 11 is the only instance of officially sponsored anti-Semitism on a national level.

There are four possible explanations for Grant's actions: The first, and simplest, is that Grant was an anti-Semite, who used the Jewish participation in the smuggling as an excuse to vent his bigotry. It's possible. Other Union generals, such as Sherman and Sheridan, did not think highly of Jews.

But before we start boycotting Grant's home in Galena, Illinois or Grant's Tomb in New York (and just who **is** buried there?), let's check out possibility Number Two: Grant was simply following the recommendations of his officers. They told him that the Jews were behind the smuggling, and that their expulsion would end that activity. Grant didn't know that the officers recommending expulsion were the same officers who made big money participating in the smuggling. They were eager to get rid of their Jewish competition, and, by influencing Grant, succeeded in doing so.

The third possibility relates to Grant's father, Jesse. Papa Grant had gotten into a business dispute with the Mack Brothers, Jewish businessmen from Cincinnati. A lawsuit had been filed. Possibly, the younger Grant was siding with his father by sticking it to the Jews.

The fourth explanation is the opposite of the third: Jesse Grant, despite his closeness with his son, was also a big pain in the neck. Jesse was always trying to take advantage of his son's position, and was always hanging out near the Union Army camp. Grant suspected that Jesse was in partnership with some of the Jewish smugglers, and was determined to teach his father a lesson. Grant didn't want to attack his father directly, so he did the next best thing: He expelled the Jews, thereby getting rid of Jesse's partners, and forcing his father out of the smuggling trade (at least temporarily).

It is quite likely that Grant's Order was the result of more than one of these four factors. Fortunately, Lincoln abrogated the Order immediately; many other illegal acts during the Civil War (not Jew-related) had to wait for the U.S. Supreme Court to strike them down.

The issue of Order No. 11 was revived six years later in the presidential campaign of 1868, between Republican Grant and Democrat Horatio Seymour. The Democrats raised Order No. 11 as proof of Grant's unfitness for the presidency. After all, a man who violates the Constitution is not qualified to be president.

This was the first time in American history that a Jewish issue had been injected into a national campaign.[1] Grant's supporters, both Jews and non-Jews, pleaded with him to speak to the issue, but the General refused. Finally, near the end of the campaign, in a letter to a Jewish supporter, Grant made his first and only public statement on Order No. 11.

"I do not pretend to sustain the Order. At the time of its publication, I was incensed by a reprimand received from Washington for permitting acts which Jews within my lines were engaged in. There were many other persons within my lines equally bad with the worst of them, but the difference was that the Jews could pass with impunity from one army to

---

1. Maybe the Democrats also thought their candidate's name would appeal to the Jews: Vote for Seymour from New York. Almost sounds like a Jewish candidate.

the other, and gold, in violation of orders, was being smuggled through the lines, at least so it was reported.

"The order was issued and sent without any reflection and without thinking of the Jews as a sect or race to themselves, but simply as persons who had successfully (I say successfully instead of persistently, because there were plenty of others within my lines who envied their success) violated an order, which greatly inured to the help of the rebels.

"Give Mr. Moses assurance that I have no prejudice against sect or race, but want each individual to be judged by his own merit. Order No. 11 does not sustain this statement, I admit, but then I do not sustain that order. It never would have been issued if it had not been telegraphed the moment it were penned, and without reflection."

Grant's semi-apology implies that, under pressure from Washington to do something about the smuggling, Grant was too eager to listen to the anti-Semitic whispers in his ear. But Grant's statement still doesn't answer the question of whether he was an anti-Semite. Since actions speak louder than words, we should look at three incidents from Grant's presidential record.

First, after winning the election in a landslide, Grant offered the important cabinet position of Treasury Secretary to Joseph Seligman, a Jewish financier who was the Haym Salomon of the Civil War. Seligman turned down Grant's offer – he couldn't afford the salary cut – but the importance lay in the offer. No Jew was to serve in the cabinet until Oscar Straus in 1906, and that was in a dinky department, Commerce and Labor. If Grant hated Jews, he would not have offered a Jew the Treasury position – unless, of course, he thought a Jew would be perfect as Treasury Secretary, since "those people" are good with money.

Second, while Grant was president, a movement to ban schechita (Jewish ritual slaughtering) was picking up steam. That movement wanted and needed Grant's support to get their anti-schechita program enacted into law. Grant, however, refused to give them his support, and their proposals never passed.

Most important of all was Grant's reaction to anti-Semitic pogroms that broke out in Romania in 1871. The United States had no diplomatic or commercial interests in Romania, and therefore had no diplomatic representation there. Benjamin Peixotto (pronounced "Pishotto"), a Jewish community leader, was determined to help his unfortunate brethren. But what could he do? Someone (perhaps Peixotto) came up with a brilliant scheme – but it would need Grant's approval.

Peixotto, using private funds, would buy a building in Romania's capital, Bucharest. He would raise the stars-and-stripes, and call the building the American consulate to Romania, with Peixotto officially appointed as U.S. Consul. Grant agreed with the plan, and appointed Peixotto Consul to Romania. Under the authority of the United States, Peixotto tried to alleviate the sufferings of the Romanian Jews.[1]

Grant's approval of the Peixotto scheme ranks as one of the most humanitarian efforts by an American president. Based on his presidential actions, Grant was no anti-Semite, and we should feel free to visit his home in Galena. Of course, this doesn't mean that Grant was not anti-Semitic in 1862, but if he had overcome and outgrown his prejudices, it is all the more to his credit.

In his memoirs, Grant discusses virtually all aspects of his Civil War experience – but there is not a word about Order No. 11. Perhaps Grant's omission is due to his shame and embarrassment over having issued that infamous Order.

After the Civil War, the United States was a divided nation, with much bitterness and anger between North and South. That was not the case, however, in the American Jewish community. The Jewish attitude was, "We will fight – and die, if need be – for our country, but we will not forget that we are part of one Jewish people." B'nai B'rith illustrated this feeling by functioning in both North and South during the war as if there were no conflict.

---

1. Peixotto's efforts were similar to those of Raul Wallenberg in 1944 Budapest. Wallenberg used the Swedish flag as his authority.

Within a month after Appomattox, Northern Jews were sending matzohs down South so that their southern brethren could observe Passover. To American Jews, when the war was over, it was over – no need to dwell in the past. An example of this is found in the Kahn family of Marshall, Texas. Emanuel Kahn had fought for the South; his brother, Lionel, had joined the Union army. After the war, the brothers returned home and went back into business together, putting the past behind them. In other cases, Jewish soldiers in the occupying Union Army would meet and marry local Jewish girls, settle down near the in-laws, and become pillars of their new community.[1]

---

1. Whoopi Goldberg's real name is Caren Johnson.

CHAPTER 4

HOW THE BUBBIES AND ZAYDIES CAME TO AMERICA

The exploits of American Jewry detailed in the past three chapters make for fascinating reading; but the ancestors of 90% of today's U.S. Jewish community didn't show up to these shores until the great migration that began in 1881. That's not to say that there were **no** Eastern European Jews in America before 1881. From 1820-1870, about 7500 Jews emigrated from that area. Another 41,000 arrived in the 1870s.

Most of these Jews came from Russia, with others emigrating from Austria-Hungary and Romania. The irony of Russian Jewry is that they never wanted to be there in the first place. As I mentioned in the Introduction, the Jews of western Europe moved into Poland in the Middle Ages. In the late 1700s, the center of Jewish life in the world was still based in that country. But through a series of partitions, Poland was wiped off the map, as Prussia, Austria-Hungary, and Russia all split it up.

Therefore, by 1795, Russia, which had had virtually no Jews, now found its western frontier filled with them. It was as if the official U.S. government policy was anti-French Canadian, filled with hatred of those people – and then, the U.S. went and annexed Quebec, bringing all those hated people within its borders.

The Jews didn't have much say in the matter, and were stuck living in the world's most anti-Semitic country. Throughout the 19th century, the community was subject to various oppressions, the worst of which was Czar Nicholas I's policy of drafting 12-year-old Jewish boys into the Russian Army. Yet, the Jews survived, and even saw a glimmer of hope under the reign óf Alexander II. Alex-2 may have been a despot and a dictator, but, by Russian standards, he was a flaming liberal. Naturally, he was assassinated in 1881.

Alex-2 was replaced by his son, Alex-3, who reasoned that reactionary Russian rulers live longer than liberals. In 1881, Russia was besieged by poverty, hunger, and a host of other problems. Alex-3 opted for the oldest solution in the book: Blame the Jews.

So it was that soon after Alex-3 took over, pogroms, encouraged by his regime, broke out throughout Russia. Dozens of Jews were killed, injured, maimed, and left homeless. We got the message: Jews by the thousands poured across the border to Austria-Hungary as the first step in a westward migration to the Promised Land (America, not Israel). Further pogroms occurred throughout the next 35 years, the worst being the one in Kishinev in 1903.

Alex-3 and his advisors also put the screws to the Jews in the economic field as well. In May, 1882, Alex-3 issued laws preventing Jews from owning or renting land; restricting Jews from certain urban areas of Russia; and establishing quotas to prevent Jews from receiving education (under the guise of affirmative action programs, no doubt). These edicts were called the May Laws after their month of passage because the Russians had no imagination to call them anything else.

The official Russian policy was summed up by one of Alex-3's ministers: One-third of the Jews will die; one-third will convert; and one-third will be forced out. Obviously, the minister knew nothing about the American Jewish experience: Had the Russians given the Jews total freedom, most of the Jews would have disappeared through intermarriage – and the Russians would have gotten to keep the Jewish brainpower.

The emigration from Russia was similar to the one from Germany 50 years earlier, in that it was the poorest and least-educated who left first. Just as the failure of the 1848 revolutions convinced the German-Jewish middle and upper-classes that there was no hope in Germany, so too, the failure of the attempt at Russian Democracy in 1905 convinced the middle and upper-class Russian Jews that they had to leave.

O.K., time for some numbers: From 1881-1924, 2-1/4 million Jews came to the United States. Jews were only a small percentage of the total immigration to America during this period. However, Jews made up a large percentage of those emigrants who left specific areas. Confused? Don't be. Here's an example of what I'm talking about: Let's look at Galicia, the large area that is located in southeastern Poland and western Ukraine. Galicia is the source of the finest, smartest, wittiest, most intellectual, and best-looking Jews in Eastern Europe, if not the world. In short, the cream of the crop.[1] Jews made up 12% of the general population of Galicia, but 60% of all emigrants from Galicia were Jews. Still confused? Re-read this paragraph – slowly, this time.

There were certain factors that distinguished Jews from the other immigrant groups: Many of the non-Jewish newcomers had arrived in America's big cities as peasants fresh off the farms. Seventy percent of the Jewish immigrants, on the other hand, had worked in some form of urban commerce or industry, mainly the needle trades. So it is no surprise that Jews gravitated to similar work when they got off the boat.

Another difference: A much larger percentage of Jews arrived in America as families, not as single young people. Either the family arrived intact, or the father came alone, working night and day to earn enough money to bring the rest of his family over.

Yet another difference: A little-known fact about the mass immigration to America is that one-third of all immigrants returned to their homelands. This was not the case with the Jews, only 5-6% of whom

---

1. This is an objective historical opinion, and has absolutely nothing to do with the fact that my parents are "Galitzianers."

returned. Why is this? The answer is obvious. A Sicilian could return to Sicily, a Pole to a Polish area (if not to an independent Polish state), but a Jew really had no place to go. Back to Russia and pogroms? No way.

The voyage to America was difficult and unpleasant. Most of the earlier immigrants had snuck out of Russia to the Austro-Hungarian city of Brody. From there, they made their way to a port city like Hamburg, and then on to America. On the boat, the immigrants did not enjoy the lovely sea air. They traveled in steerage, which was sort of like traveling to America on a subway train during rush hour.

On board, the food was bad, but since it wasn't kosher, most Jews didn't touch it anyway. They lived, instead, on black bread, herring and tea for the 10-14 day voyage. Ironically, steerage was created by a German Jew named Albert Ballin, head of the Hamburg-America Line. His ships used to carry materials such as timber in the cargo hold from America to Europe, but would make the voyage westward empty. It was Ballin who came up with the concept of filling the empty cargo holds with people. Ballin is thus the inspiration behind today's cheap, overcrowded charter flights.

The boats, containing insufficient toilets, soon smelled worse than New Jersey on a bad day. All this, plus the usual Atlantic Ocean rocking and rolling, led to seasickness among virtually all the passengers. I think that the term "greener," for new immigrants, doesn't come from the word "greenhorn," but probably derives from the newcomers' skin color when they disembarked (or "deboated" to use a modern mangling of the English language). Also, based on the conditions of passage, I can't believe that **any** immigrant came to America overweight.

The immigrants' anxieties didn't end with their arrival. They were crowded into the massive reception area in Ellis Island, surrounded by unfriendly immigration officers whose language they barely understood, if at all. There was also the fear of being rejected due to diseases such as trachoma (which is some sort of eye problem). In later years, personnel of Jewish relief organizations were stationed at Ellis Island to assist the newcomers and calm their fears.

So now our immigrants have overcome the obstacles by bounding the borders, sailing the sea (while barfing the black bread), and passing the inspections (I ran out of alliterations). Next stop: The Lower East Side.

Today, through the rose-colored glasses of nostalgia (or the blu-blockers of bad memories), it's easy to romanticize the Lower East Side as the place where the bubbies and zaydies (grandmas and grandpas) worked hard to become Americans and lived in harmony with other hard-working, poor-but-proud Jews. In reality, the Lower East Side was an overcrowded slum. In fact, at the turn of the century, the L.E.S. was the most densely populated neighborhood in the world, except possibly for Calcutta or Bombay. Some blocks had over 1,000 people per acre. The best way to get a feel for the old L.E.S. is to rent the movie "Hester Street." More than any book, that film recreates the neighborhood with all its congestion and other problems.

The Jews of the Lower East Side grouped themselves according to their area of origin. Hungarians lived north of Houston Street;[1] Galitzianers were found between Houston and Broome; Romanians from Chrystie to Allen; and the tiny group of Sephardim lived near the Romanians.[2]

Many of the L.E.S. residents lived in buildings called "dumbbell tenements." Not surprisingly, a bird's eye view of those structures would show that they were indeed shaped like dumbbells, wide at the ends and narrow in the middle. That shape won an award for design in a competition for best building for low-income housing. Unfortunately, the design didn't work quite so well when hundreds of these buildings were erected one on top of the other. There was no light because of the crowding. The narrow part in the middle allowed fires and filth to sweep upwards. There weren't

---

1. Pronounced just like it's spelled, not "Yooston." Saying "Yooston" instead of "Houston" is as sure a sign of being a tourist as saying "Avenue of the Americas" instead of "Sixth Avenue."
2. Those poor Sephardim. Their ignorance of Yiddish made them not-quite-Jewish in their neighbors' eyes.

enough toilet facilities in the building. Of course, it could have been worse; at least they weren't living in a 1990s public housing project.

Yet, despite living in crowded unsanitary conditions, the Jews of the Lower East Side, had the lowest mortality rate in New York. Aha! Another argument for Jewish superiority, we cry. But what were the objective reasons for the low mortality rate?

First, there were a lot of medical facilities in the L.E.S. A number of immigrants were doctors, and practiced in their own neighborhood. Also, the German Jews had set up clinics in the area, which the poor Jews took great advantage of (a grammatically incorrect sentence, but it sounds better).

Second, the Jews never stayed encased in filth for very long. At least once a week (usually for the Sabbath), Jewish men would head for the schvitz, the steambaths of the neighborhood. The steam and showers would open their pores and clean them out, without having to waste time showing off on the Stairmaster or Lifecycle. Women went to the schvitz in lesser numbers, but those who remained religious went to the ritual bath once a month. (I won't get into a discussion of the laws of family purity, which are either primitive or beautiful, depending on your religious orientation.)

The third explanation relates to what Jews ate and drank. Although the kosher laws have absolutely nothing to do with health (otherwise, Jews would be big and strong and non-Jews would be shrimpy and near-sighted), keeping kosher did reduce the extent of tainted food that Jews ate. As for drink, Jews didn't – at least, not too much. No booze, so no liver ailments, no drunken brawls, and no beer commercials featuring the Lower East Side bikini team. But more on booze later.

Despite their relative good physical health, the Jews led the way in other diseases. Jews had a very high rate of hypertension, ulcers, and other diseases showing a nervous condition. In other words, the Jewish community of the Lower East Side was stressed out like crazy. In that respect, Jews haven't changed. We're still filled with nervousness and anxieties. That's why we produce all the great comedians. Psychologically,

Woody Allen (when he was still funny) and Richard Lewis would have fit perfectly in the Lower East Side.

One result of the stress (and a cause of even more stress) was the high divorce and desertion rate in the L.E.S. One cause of divorce was shown in "Hester Street." A husband would immigrate first, become Americanized, and a few years later, be re-united with his "backwards" wife. Another cause was the boarder. Many renters would take in boarders to help out with the finances. If a wife was still in Europe, the boarder and his/her landlady/landlord would find themselves in a more-than-business relationship. At least with a divorce, a wife knew where she stood. If she was deserted, her life was in limbo. She was neither divorcee nor widow, and could not re-marry and get on with her life.

The Immigrants' Jobs – "Nem dus Arbeit and Shove It"

The immigrants gravitated to the garment business, which for decades was a Jewish-controlled industry. Why? Four reasons (which must be memorized for the final exam):

1) Many Jews had obtained experience in this field back in Russia. You do what you know, and they knew sewing/tailoring/stitching.

2) The field was cheap to get into. Unlike a store, an immigrant didn't have to spend a lot of money on merchandise. For the garment business, he only needed a sewing machine. Later, with the rise of the factory system, he (or she) didn't even need that.

3) The bosses were Jews. Of course, these were German Jews, whom the Russians viewed as only one step removed from Protestants, but Jews all the same. "Better to work for one of ours than a goy," they figured.

4) Under the contractor system, a worker took home pieces of material, and was paid for each skirt or blouse or suit he made. The advantage of this system was that a worker could make his own hours, and therefore, did not have to violate the Sabbath. A store, on the other

hand, was hard to keep closed on Saturdays, especially with local Blue Laws mandating Sunday closings.

The working conditions in the garment business were miserable, at best. Take a worker, for example, who worked as a contract laborer in his apartment. First, the apartment itself was a dark, stuffy slum with poor sanitary conditions. Next, the payment for each piece was very little, so the worker had to make as many garments as possible. He did this by enlisting the entire family to do the work, from little kids to old bubbies. They all spent their days hunched over sewing machines or working with needle and thread in their poorly-lit dwelling.

The contractor system was replaced by the more efficient factory. Conditions improved very little, as the workers traded their independence for wage slavery. The factories were noisy, stuffy, and crowded. The hours were long, and if you didn't come in on Saturday, you needn't come in on Monday. All these factors led to the great labor tragedy known as the Triangle fire.

The Triangle Shirtwaist Company was housed in a big building near Greenwich Village. Naturally, the company made shirtwaists. You don't know what a shirtwaist is? Neither did I. The dictionary says it's a dress whose top is shaped like a shirt. Anyway, in 1911, hundreds of immigrant girls, mostly Jews and Italians, worked for Triangle. The factory was so stuffy and crowded that the girls would go on the fire escape for a smoke during breaks. The bosses felt that the girls were taking extra-long breaks. To prevent the loss of a precious five minutes or so of extra work time, the bosses locked all the fire escape doors.

One day, a fire started in the factory. With all the bits of material lying around, it spread quickly. The girls in the upper floors frantically tried to get out, but the doors to safety were locked. The girls who weren't burned to death or choked by the smoke died when they jumped the 11 stories to the ground. When it was all over, 145 girls were dead.

Memorial meetings were held, announced by signs in English, Yiddish and Italian. The bosses, who by all rights should have been hung by their urethras, hired a good lawyer, who got them off. But the tragedy at least led to reforms in the conditions of factories that helped improve the lot of the immigrant worker.

Ironically, the major improvement in the workers' conditions had occurred the year before the Triangle fire. In 1910, the Jewish labor unions had called a mass strike, protesting poor working conditions and low wages. Both the workers and management dug in their heels. A 54-year-old nationally prominent Jewish lawyer with no prior involvement with the Jewish community was called upon to mediate the dispute. Louis Brandeis succeeded in getting the two sides together, and agreeing to an historic accord, giving the union much of what they had asked for. Brandeis not only emerged as a hero to the masses, but the mediation had kindled his dormant Jewish feelings. From that point on, he would become more and more involved in Jewish affairs.

Crime Among the Jews – Nu, So I'll Make You an Offer You Can't Refuse

As we all know, from listening to sociologists, criminologists, urbanologists, and proctologists,[1] crime is a direct result of poverty and poor living conditions. Well, based on that, the Lower East Side and Chicago's Maxwell Street should have been hotbeds of criminal activity. Were they?

The answer is Yes, according to New York City Police Commissioner Theodore Bingham. In a 1908 magazine article, Bingham claimed that Jews were responsible for 50% of all crime in the city. That article caused a furor, with Bingham, accused of anti-Semitism, forced to retract some of his charges. But was he right? Were Jews really responsible for half of New York's crime?

It depends on what you consider "crime." Jews were massive violators of New York's Blue Laws, that is, those laws that required a business to shut down on Sunday. If "crime" includes tickets issued for Blue Law

---

1. Just wanted to make sure you were still paying attention.

violations, then Jews could very well have been responsible for 50% of all crime.

But what about real crime, the kind we associate with slums today? In 1898, Jews had the lowest rate in the U.S. for violent crimes. Jewish crime tended to be economic: Embezzlement, forgery, fraud. Jews, for the most part, did not go around mugging, shooting, or assaulting people. By today's standards, the Lower East Side, and other immigrant Jewish neighborhoods, were very safe places. One reason was the relative lack of bars. Drinking leads to fighting, and fighting leads to smashing someone's head in. With fewer saloons, there were fewer heads smashed in.

The other reason is the chauvinistic, ethnic one. Hey! We're Jews. We just don't go around beating people up. To quote Jackie Mason, in a Jewish neighborhood, you're not afraid you're going to be mugged by an accountant. Likewise, at the turn of the century, you weren't afraid of getting mugged by the accountant's grandfather either.

However, what about buying sex from the accountant's grandmother? What! You don't mean to imply that there was [whisper] prostitution on the Lower East Side? Damn right there was, and lots of it, too. Allen Street was lined with bordellos. Don't be so surprised. Many women were living in poverty, especially widows, divorcees, or those abandoned by their husbands. Without skills, they sometimes turned to the oldest profession. This topic has always been hushed up, but if we understand its causes, we will understand why there has been an upsurge of prostitution in Israel among Russian immigrants who are in the same situation as those women of a century ago.

Prostitution among American Jewish women was not unknown even before the great immigration. Out west, there were many Jewish prostitutes. However, they viewed the profession as a temporary one, until they made enough money to do something better. And plenty of them made good money. It seems that Jewish prostitutes were considered a luxury item. Even more so, Jewish prostitutes with red hair.

Many of these Jewish girls quickly went from being workers to entering the ranks of management; that is, they became madams. There was much jealousy of the Jewish girls then. Unlike the non-Jewish prostitutes, the Jewish girls "graduated," and didn't stay in the business until their teeth fell out and they died of venereal disease.

Unfortunately, we don't have statistics to tell us what happened to the Jewish prostitutes of the Lower East Side, but if they were anything like other immigrant Jews, their years in that business were few, and their grandchildren are today suburban professionals (no, not the same kind of professional).[1]

That leaves us with one other criminal type: The mob guy. As everyone knows (even before the movie "Bugsy"), there were many Jews in the ranks of organized crime. But again, there was a difference between Jewish mobsters and non-Jewish mobsters.

First, there were no Jewish crime "families." Usually, the Jewish mobster was the only one of his family to enter that particular profession. One of the most vicious criminals, Louie "Lepke" Buchhalter, had several brothers and sisters, all of whom lived quite respectable lives.

Another distinction was that Jewish crime was usually a one-generational affair. Mobsters viewed their activities as a profitable business, but not one they would ever want their children to enter. Like all Jewish parents, they were in a particular livelihood to achieve middle-class status and to enable their children to do better. Unfortunately, we don't know whether their children did indeed lead better, more respectable lives.[2]

---

1. Ph.D. alert: This paragraph may be used as an inspiration for a doctoral dissertation on the topic, "Post-Prostitution Activities of Jewish Women on the Lower East Side."
2. Another Ph.D. alert: This paragraph may be used as inspiration for a dissertation on the topic, "Mobility Among Children of Jewish Organized Crime Figures."

Education – Is All A's the Best You Could Do?

The common denominator among the immigrant Jews was the desire for upward mobility. For some Jews, the means to that end was crime. For most Jews, though, it was education.

Jewish parents realized early on that the key to their kids' success was education. They imparted this attitude to their children, and, as a result, the immigrant children became very serious students. Of course, this emphasis on education was nothing new. It was ingrained in the Jewish psyche for thousands of years. It may have also been ingrained genetically. Among Jews, the richest men in town married their daughters off to the brightest students in town, who passed this stress on academic excellence to their children. In Catholicism, on the other hand, the brightest students became priests, who tried unsuccessfully to pass their love of learning to bored parishioners.

Teachers were the new nobility of the Lower East Side. For years, these educators, mostly Irish women, were forced to deal with classes of students who weren't all that interested in what they had to teach. But now, with the arrival of the Jewish immigrants, those teachers saw themselves raised to the level of demi-gods. The children hung on the teacher's every word, determined to excel in their studies. Immigrant accounts vary as to whether the teachers loved or hated their new students. While it is impossible to generalize, I'm sure that most of the teachers loved the immigrant children for at least one reason: They probably couldn't help but feel affection for the people who gave them so much respect and admiration.

Another indication of the children's seriousness was the public library in the Lower East Side: It was crowded from morning to night. Jewish love of books hasn't changed over the past century. In my own village of Skokie, Illinois, the library has many patrons waiting for its doors to open on Sunday mornings, and the place is always packed with Jews and Orientals (our successors, as I'll discuss later on).

As early as 1888, 25% of City College's graduating class was Jewish, but that was only the beginning, as Jews would explode on the college scene over the next 30 years. On the secondary level, 53% of all New York City high school students in 1918 were Jewish.

Germans vs. Russians – Apostates vs. Primitives

Many of the old-line German Jews looked upon the newcomers with disgust. The Germans were wealthy, cultured people, possessors of the best of German and American culture, modern enough to believe in Classical Reform, the Judaism with no Jewish content. They were respectable, and could easily mix in Gentile circles.

But **these people** from off the boat! They were primitive, uncouth, superstitious. To the Germans, the Russians were the black sheep invading America. Even worse, there were so many of them. By 1910, the percentage of Germans among Jews in New York had shrunk to only 10%. The Germans were determined not to let the Russians mingle with them, and kept them out of their clubs. The unofficial slogan of the German-Jewish Harmony Club was "More polish and less Polish."

The Russians hated the Germans right back. Their German cousins were hardly worth calling Jews. They practiced a religion that couldn't truly be called Judaism, and were all a bunch of snobs who cared more about wealth and outward appearances than their fellow Jews. But that wasn't surprising, considering that their goal was to become Episcopalians.

Some German communal leaders rose above these petty feelings, and were determined to help the "downtown" Jews. The leader of this effort was the great Jacob Schiff (1847-1920), a man who had his hand in virtually every Jewish community endeavor for 50 years. He convinced other wealthy Germans that if they led the effort to Americanize the immigrants, the Russians would become as respectable as the old-timers. The desire on the part of the Germans to Americanize the Russians had its Catholic counterpart. The Irish led the way in the Americanization of Poles and Italians. After all, they, the Irish, did not want the Catholic church to be viewed as an un-American foreign entity.

Schiff helped break down the barriers between the two groups, and led in the formation of educational and charitable institutions on the Lower East Side. One of those institutions, the Educational Alliance, became the center for adult education and athletic activities among the immigrants. Schiff himself felt closer to the immigrants than his fellow Germans, perhaps because he had a traditional streak to him. Despite his having been president of Reform Temple Emanu-El, Schiff always said the mourner's prayer (kaddish) for his parents in Orthodox Beis Medrash Hagadol on the Lower East Side. Unfortunately, there has never been a proper biography written about Schiff.[1]

Within a few years, the immigrants began earning enough money to look beyond the Lower East Side. The outer boroughs had wider streets, more park area, and bigger and newer apartments. So it was that areas of the Bronx and Brooklyn became as Jewish as the Lower East Side. The same pattern held true for other cities, like Chicago, where the Jews abandoned Maxwell Street for the broad boulevards of the West Side Lawndale area. These new neighborhoods were to survive until the mid-1950s.

One side effect of Americanization and upward mobility was the loss of religion. In "Word of Our Fathers," Irving Howe implies that most of the immigrants were socialist firebrands who had given up on religion in Europe. But, in fact, most were average religious Jews, who were forced to give up religious observance due to the economic necessities of life in the U.S. With the father working on the Sabbath, and the children in the Americanizing blender of the public schools, it was impossible to transmit traditional Judaism to the next generation.

There were other reasons as well. Some Jews openly rebelled against religion. Those included Howe's socialists, as well as people who had felt stifled by religion in Russia, and gloried in the freedom of America. Finally, with most Orthodox leaders in Europe telling their congregations that

---

1. Prominent American Jewish historian, Naomi W. Cohen, the person best qualified to write a Schiff bio, informed me that she is now working on that project.

America was "trefe" (non-kosher) and to be avoided at all costs, the cream of the Orthodox intelligentsia was not to be found in the U.S. In fact, the rabbis and teachers of the immigrant generation were of such low quality, that they probably did more to turn off the entire younger generation of American Jews than any other single factor.

Despite any loss of religious observance, however, no immigrant would think of turning to Reform. They all considered it virtually another religion, the Protestant-like faith of the despised Germans. But were the immigrants correct in that assumption? To see, we must review the histories of all three branches of Judaism at the time.

Reform/Conservative/Orthodox and How They Got That Way

Reform

By 1880, before the Russian immigration wave, Reform was triumphant, with 90% of all American synagogues affiliated with that movement. In 1885, in Pittsburgh, the Reform movement issued its platform of principles. The document was influenced by David Einhorn's radical sons-in-law, Kaufman Kohler and Emil Hirsch. Isaac Mayer Wise went along for unity's sake, saying "I was for this platform all along."

In short, the Pittsburgh Platform stated that only Judaism's moral and ethical laws were still applicable; any ritual laws, like kashrut and the Sabbath were ancient and irrelevant. It was also strongly anti-nationalistic. We don't need a country in Palestine; America is our Zion, and Washington is our Jerusalem.

Emil Hirsch, of Chicago's Temple Sinai, went even further: His congregation held services on Sunday. The benefit of that, besides not interfering with the work week, was that it was another turn-off to any nouveau riche Russian Jew who might think of social-climbing by joining the temple. Hirsch despised those people.

There's an apocryphal story that I heard several years ago at University of Chicago Law School. When future attorney-general Edward

Levi was dean of the Law School, a religious Jewish student informed him that a final exam was scheduled for the holiday of Shavuot, when writing is prohibited. Could he have the exam re-scheduled? Levi thought for a moment, and replied, "Shavuot is the holiday commemorating the giving of the law. What more perfect day is there for taking a law exam?" Levi is Hirsch's grandson. If this story is true, it would show the true spirit of Hirsch lived on for another couple of generations.

Classical Reform was religion without any soul. Increasingly, questions were raised whether there was any difference between Reform and Unitarianism. Reformers fended off that issue by stating that Unitarianism, for all its theological blandness, stemmed from Christianity, leading to essential differences between the two faiths. The exact nature of those differences remained uncertain.

Another challenge was not so easily dismissed. Felix Adler, son of the rabbi of New York's Temple Emanu-El, was being groomed to take his father's place. Instead, Adler rejected Reform, and founded the Society for Ethical Culture. E.C. was Reform without even its little bit of Judaism; a sort of do-good religion that would have blossomed in Southern California. Many Reform lay leaders joined Adler, while remaining within Reform. Classical Reform had no answer to Adler's "ethical" challenge, and it would be forced to wrestle theologically with that issue until Reform itself would re-discover Judaism in the late 20th century.

As the years went on, Reform leaders began to reject the Pittsburgh Platform's anti-nationalistic plank. One of the earliest dissenters was the aged Bernhard Felsenthal of Chicago, who, in the late 1890s, was issued membership No. 1 in the Chicago Zionist chapter. Later, Reform rabbis Richard Gottheil, Judah Magnes, Stephen Wise, and Abba Hillel Silver became the leaders of American Zionism. It was not until 1937, however, that Reform officially adopted the pro-Zionist Columbus Platform.

By the 1880s, under Isaac Mayer Wise's leadership, Reform had established its congregational organization (Union of American Hebrew Congregations) and its rabbinical group (Central Conference of American

Rabbis). In 1875, Wise had founded a rabbinical school in Cincinnati called Hebrew Union College. The first class was set to graduate in 1883.

At that time, while there were lines drawn between Reformers and Traditionalists, those lines were not set in stone. In fact, the Traditionalists, led by Hazzan Sabato Morais of Philadelphia, were willing to give Wise's institution a chance. A number of them were guests at the first graduation. A graduation dinner was served, which the guests assumed would be kosher. However, they looked down at their plates, and, to their dismay, saw shellfish staring back at them.

The Traditionalists were insulted and angered (not to mention hungry). They walked out, convinced that the breach between them and Reform was now total. The Traditionalists realized that they would have to set up their own institutions in America to survive.

Conservative

A common question: If Conservative Judaism is more liberal than Orthodoxy, then why is it called Conservative? Because it was the conservative reaction to Reform Judaism, specifically to the "trefe [non-kosher] banquet" at the Hebrew Union College graduation.

The original ideas behind Conservatism were first developed in Germany by Rabbi Zecharia Frankel, who called for changes in Jewish practices, but within the Halacha (Jewish law). Frankel called his theory "Positive-Historical Judaism," a typically ponderous German title (from those same folks who brought you "Wissenschaft des Judentums," "Weltanschauung" and other names sprinkled liberally in students' answers to history essay questions).

In January, 1887, ten anti-Reform religious leaders founded the Jewish Theological Seminary of America. The ten were a mixed group of five Traditionalists and five moderate Reformers (who thought the Pittsburgh Platform had gone too far). The synagogues that supported JTS ranged from Orthodox Beis Medrash Hagadol to Reform Shaaray Tefila.

Originally, JTS was an Orthodox institution, as was its president, Sabato Morais of Philadelphia's Mikveh Israel. Even the right-wing rabbinical group, Agudas Harabbonim, considered the first 17 rabbis ordained by JTS (through 1902) as Orthodox. In fact, the first JTS graduate is probably the most famous of this early group: Joseph Hertz ('94), the future British Chief Rabbi, whose Hertz Pentateuch is a standard feature of Orthodox and Conservative synagogues today.

The early JTS, however, was a weak institution. Caught between the Yiddish-speaking Orthodox of the Lower East Side and the too-cool-for-real-Judaism Reformers of Uptown, JTS found it hard to place its graduates or to raise sufficient funds. Things got worse after 1897, when Morais died, leaving JTS leader-less.

Things changed in 1901: Cyrus Adler, a member of the JTS board, had a meeting with Jacob Schiff, telling him of the school's problems. "Surely, Mr. Schiff, you realize the importance of modern religious leadership for the immigrant masses of the Lower East Side. That leadership will come neither from the old Yiddish rabbis nor the Uptown Reformers. JTS can provide that leadership – if it has the money."

Schiff enthusiastically took the fundraising challenge upon himself. He got his German friends to also contribute, and within a short time, JTS had all the money it needed (if only things were that easy with my kids' day school). From the start, Adler and Schiff had only one person in mind to head JTS: Solomon Schechter of Cambridge University in England.

Schechter had been a well-known scholar within academic circles. However, after he discovered the Cairo Geniza, with its boxloads of rare Jewish documents, his fame became widespread. When offered the position, Schechter didn't have to think twice. He told Adler that despite his success in Europe, he looked forward to going to New York, because "If I can make it there, I can make it anywhere."

Schechter reorganized JTS, bringing on board scholars like Louis Ginzberg and Israel Friedlaender. He also moved the school out of the Orthodox world, and formed a new one: American Conservative Judaism, in which Halacha had a strong say in religious practices, but not a veto. Thus, Schechter tried to stake out the middle ground between Orthodoxy and Reform.

On a personal level, Schechter got along much better with Reform rabbis than Orthodox ones. Orthodoxy may have made him feel uncomfortable, because it represented his own background, from which he had moved away. On the other hand, many in Orthodoxy distrusted his innovations, viewing Schechter as a heretic. In fact, for years, JTS was known in Orthodox circles as "Schechter's school."

One distinguishing factor of Conservatism, unlike the other branches, was its enthusiasm for Zionism. Schechter was especially pro-Zionist, and eventually had a falling-out with Schiff over the issue. Schiff, like many other German Jews of his era, remained unsympathetic to Zionism until World War One.

Schechter went on to establish Conservatism's rabbinical group (Rabbinical Assembly) and its congregational organization (United Synagogue of America). He died in 1915, never having totally recovered from spending all that time in the dusty attic of the Cairo Geniza.

Schechter was replaced by Cyrus Adler, who remained JTS president until 1940. Adler was one of the most important figures in the American Jewish community, with his fingers in just about every Jewish pie. While serving as JTS president, he was also president of Dropsie University in Philadelphia, editor of the American Jewish Yearbook, and a key member of a whole host of organizations, including the American Jewish Historical Society and the Jewish Publication Society. The Arkansas-born Adler was one of a group of Philadelphia Jewish leaders who exerted great influence over the entire American Jewish community.[1]

In 1940, Adler died and was replaced by JTS alumnus Louis Finkelstein, who would lead the school for over three decades. Finkelstein, a prominent scholar, was a star fund-raiser, and he established JTS as a premier institution of Jewish research in the United States.

---

1. Others included Isaac Leeser, Sabato Morais, Cyrus Sulzberger, Solomon Solis-Cohen, and Bernard Levinthal.

Orthodox

If Orthodoxy is viewed as traditional Judaism, then it can be said that all the early American synagogues were Orthodox, albeit of the Sephardic tradition. In fact, to Sephardim, Orthodoxy equals Judaism. A Jew may be more religious or less religious, but never Reform.

The Orthodoxy I am discussing here, however, is that of Eastern Europe. The main Orthodox synagogue in New York when the Russian Jews arrived was Beis Medrash Hagadol, led by Rabbi Abraham Asch. When Asch died in 1887, a group of laymen decided that what the anarchic American community needed was a chief rabbi. They found their man in Rabbi Jacob Joseph of Vilna. Of course, not everyone thought Rabbi Joseph was needed. The Germans of Uptown and the Socialists of Downtown were both derisive of the very idea of a chief rabbi in the Land of the Free.

In 1888, Joseph came to America. He surprised everyone with his sincerity and personality, and even made a favorable impression upon the Germans. He attended funerals of union members, and presented himself as a communal leader. Unfortunately, the honeymoon did not last. First, the Lower East Side had plenty of other rabbis who wanted to be the "chief." In fact, some of them even began calling themselves "chief rabbi" as well. A story was told about a storefront synagogue that had a sign in the window declaring the proprietor, "Chief Rabbi of America." When asked who made him the chief rabbi, the man replied, "The sign painter."

A more serious problem arose over the question of kashrut supervision. One of Rabbi Joseph's tasks was to bring order out of chaos in the kosher meat industry by being the sole kosher certifier. To pay for this operation, he would levy a tax of one cent on each piece of meat. But Joseph was undercut by other rabbis who were willing to charge even less, and to overlook infractions of the kosher laws. Soon the powerful butchers, looking to their profits, betrayed Joseph by refusing to pay his salary.

Joseph tried to fight back, but his allies were outnumbered. In 1897, he suffered a stroke, leaving him paralyzed until his death in 1902. His death induced strong guilt feelings among the population of the Lower East Side. Out of guilt – and respect – 100,000 people attended his funeral.

Chicago Orthodoxy is always a few years behind that of New York.[1] This was true concerning the chief rabbi idea as well. In 1902 Rabbi Judah David Willowski (known as the Ridbaz) was brought to Chicago to be its Chief Rabbi. However, Rabbi Simon H. Album, who already considered himself the city's chief rabbi, fought against Willowski, gaining the butchers' support. Unlike Rabbi Joseph, who fought back until his health was broken, Willowski was more realistic. After a year, he said, "The hell with all of you," (in Yiddish of course) and left Chicago, never to return.

Almost unnoticed in New York, in 1886, was the founding of Etz Chaim, a Jewish elementary school. Eleven years later, in 1897, another group established a more advanced institution, the Rabbi Isaac Elchanan Theological Seminary. RIETS's main goal then was not to ordain rabbis, but to give immigrants a place to learn Talmud. Etz Chaim's early history proceeded uneventfully. Not so RIETS. In 1906, there was a student strike calling for the introduction of some secular subjects in the RIETS curriculum. The strike almost destroyed the school, and drove many of the more promising students (such as Solomon Goldman) to the stability of JTS.

In 1915, in an unusual burst of communal sanity, leaders of Etz Chaim and RIETS merged the two schools. Etz Chaim became the Talmudical Academy, the first Jewish high school combining secular and religious studies (and my high school alma mater, class of '72). RIETS became TA's graduate rabbinical seminary. The leader of the merged schools was Bernard Revel, the single greatest Orthodox Jewish leader in American history (and the only Jewish religious leader to get his own postage stamp, which you might have missed because it was for a buck, and who uses dollar stamps?)

Revel was a genius who received rabbinic ordination as a teenager. He came to America, and within a few years earned a Ph.D. from Dropsie. He then went into his in-laws' oil business in Oklahoma, returning to New

---

1. For example, New York's Beis Medrash Hagadol was founded in 1852; Chicago's Beis Medrash Hagadol was founded in 1866. New York's Yeshiva Etz Chaim was founded in 1886; Chicago's Yeshiva Etz Chaim was founded in 1899.

York to accept the RIETS presidency. Revel had a vision of an institution that would combine religious and secular studies on a higher level than that of TA. In 1928, he achieved his goal, and Yeshiva College was opened (yes, I went there too, class of '76).

Eventually, Yeshiva became a university, adding medical, law, business, and other graduate schools, as well as a women's college (a quaint notion in this day and age, but almost feminist in a way). Unfortunately, Revel did not live to see all this. He died young in 1940. His successor, Samuel Belkin, followed in Revel's footsteps: Another genius from Europe, who earned a Ph.D. (from Brown) soon after his arrival in America, he was dedicated to the Yeshiva ideal of the synthesis of religious and secular learning.

As for American Orthodoxy as a whole, it also developed the same organizational groups as Reform and Conservatism. In 1902, Rev. Dr.[1] Henry Pereira Mendes of Shearith Israel founded the Union of Orthodox Jewish Congregations. As for the Orthodox rabbinical group, in 1902, the Yiddish-speaking rabbis of the Lower East Side formed Agudas Harabbonim (the Union of Orthodox Rabbis). Over the years, that group proved to be too right-wing for the new graduates of Yeshiva/RIETS (as well as graduates from Chicago's Hebrew Theological College). In 1935, the younger rabbis founded the Rabbinical Council of America, representing modern Orthodox rabbis.

In Chapter 8, I will discuss the more recent history of Reform, Conservatism, and Orthodoxy, as well as Reconstructionism.

---

1. Here I mean a real doctor. Mendes had had fights with the Shearith Israel board. So he went to medical school, and let the board know that if they wanted to fire him, that was OK, because he always had medicine to fall back on. Guess what? They never fired him, possibly because you can fire a rabbi, but a doctor? Never.

CHAPTER 5

THE IMMIGRANTS SETTLE IN

Zionism in America –

Let's Help Palestine By Not Moving There

Modern Zionism was brought to America with the Russian immigrants. Despite the burst of enthusiasm that followed Herzl's convening of the First Zionist Congress in 1897, Zionists remained a tiny minority of American Jews. The Germans hated it because of Reform's anti-nationalist ideology, and because they feared the charge of dual loyalty. The immigrant Socialists were as anti-nationalistic as the Germans, believing in universal class struggle. The average Jew was sympathetic, but had no time to spend on Zionist activities; making a living took enough of his time as it was.

The Zionists made up for their small numbers by dividing into several factions: General Zionists, Labor Zionists, Religious Zionists, and Hard-Up-Guys-Who-Want-To-Meet-Girls-At-Zionist-Meeting-Zionists. These groups all practiced "Mom-and-Pop" Zionism. They didn't keep very good books, they didn't keep track of their members, and they didn't send informational material out on time, if at all. In general, the Zionist groups operated with the formality of a neighborhood candy store.

The umbrella organization of all these groups was the Federation of American Zionists, a weak association, with little money and few members. To the Zionists' surprise and joy, Louis Brandeis, still a hero due to the 1910 labor settlement he had achieved, asked to attend the FAZ national convention in 1914. At that meeting, the Zionist members overwhelmingly chose Brandeis to head the FAZ. They thought that they'd keep running American Zionism in the same slipshod manner, but with a figurehead like Brandeis at the top, they would also attract many more members.

But, as the meeting ended, and the delegates prepared to leave, they were stopped by Brandeis. "Oh, boys, before you leave, I'd like to see your books."

"Books? What books?"

"I'd also like to see your membership lists."

"Lists? What lists?"

When Brandeis heard this, he put his head in his hand (like Uncle Bill in "Family Affair," after learning about Buffy's drug problem). He told the delegates that from now on, he was running the show, and things would be different. Brandeis demanded an accurate accounting of funds and members. The delegates grumbled, but did what they were told.

Brandeis decided that he needed allies in his efficiency campaign, so he convinced his friends to join the Zionist movement. The most prominent of these was Julian Mack, a U.S. Court of Appeals judge and professor at University of Chicago Law School.

The importance of Brandeis to the fledgling American Zionist movement cannot be overstated. He single-handedly ended the dual loyalty fear among most Jews. He said that to be a good Zionist was to be a good American, because Zionism stood for the same ideals that made America great. If Louis Brandeis, the American-born, Harvard-educated advisor to President Wilson, could say that, than it must be true. Brandeis' prestige and organizational abilities helped the Zionist movement rise from an insignificant minority among a minority to a mass movement, with hundreds of thousands of members and millions of dollars in the bank.

For his part, Brandeis loved the adulation of the Jewish masses. The Boston WASP elite, in whose circles he had traveled, rejected him as both a radical and a Jew. Brandeis thought that the WASPs had turned their backs on their Pilgrim heritage. The true descendants of the American forefathers, he believed, were the poor immigrant Jews, with their egalitarian, progressive ideals.

In 1916, Brandeis was appointed as the first Jewish Supreme Court Justice; consequently, he resigned as president of the Zionist Organization of America (the FAZ's new name) replaced by Julian Mack. But the resignation was just for appearance's sake. Brandeis remained firmly in control behind the scenes.

The crowning triumph of early American Zionism was helping influence President Wilson to support the Balfour Declaration. England would not issue that document unless it was assured of Wilson's backing. Brandeis overcame Secretary of State Lansing[1] and Wilson's advisor Colonel House, to win the president's heart. Partly due to Brandeis's successes, American Jewish leaders who had been anti-Zionist, like Jacob Schiff and Louis Marshall, had, for the most part, shifted their views to **non**-Zionism.

American Zionism was so successful that it took American Jews until 1921 to do a double take, and say, "Hey, we're self-destructive American Jews with a successful program. We've got to find a way to screw it up." And they did.

Many Jews felt that Brandeis had made American Zionism **too** American, with its emphasis on economic efficiency and modern business methods. Brandeis wanted funds to be targeted towards specific projects, not collected in one mass pool of money; European Zionists felt that there was a lack of ideological fervor to Brandeisian Zionism, nothing with which to rally the troops. Finally, there was personal animosity between Brandeis

---

1. The State Department strikes again.

and Chaim Weizmann, the leader of the World Zionist Organization. Weizmann had gone back on a promise he had made to Brandeis, and the American never forgave him.

In 1921, there was a showdown at the Zionist Convention in Cleveland between Brandeis and Weizmann, economy versus ideology. The Brandeis forces were decisively defeated, but it was a Pyrrhic victory (look it up). Zionism was once again being run by business incompetents, and the movement began losing members. By 1930, it was back to pre-Brandeis numbers. Weizmann realized his mistake, and the Brandeis forces were asked back. Once again, the all-American way of doing things was applied to American Zionism.[1]

We can see this split in Zionist thought today. Groups such as the United Jewish Appeal, American Jewish Committee, and most other mainstream American Jewish organizations (even including local Federations) are run efficiently, not wasting any money. Organizations run through Israel exemplify the Weizmann forces of 1921: The Jewish Agency or any Israeli cabinet ministry is a cesspool of waste and political corruption, with millions flushed down the toilet. Someday, the efficient ideas of Brandeisian Zionism will be adopted in Israel, too – when the Messiah rides into Jerusalem on a donkey.

The Rise of American Anti-Semitism: Was It Something We Said?

Social Anti-Semitism

Before the Civil War, the United States was remarkably free of anti-Semitism. Jews were viewed more as objects of curiosity than as objects

---

1. One of those all-American ideas was the belief that Zionism consisted of the raising of funds to help someone else move to Israel. As.for American Jews' moving there, no way.

of hate. The Civil War, as we saw earlier, released the genie of anti-Semitism out of the bottle – and that genie is very hard to put back in.

First came the rise of social anti-Semitism. After the Civil War, many people joined the ranks of the wealthy through the fields of finance, real estate investing, and various entrepreneurial enterprises. If a lot of people now had money, how could the "upper" classes truly distinguish themselves? By keeping out the invaders, those nouveau riche who wanted to join them. How do you distinguish between the different classes of the nouveau riche? Easy. Just keep out the Jews.

The most famous case of Jew-exclusion occurred in 1877. Joseph Seligman, the famous financier, who had been asked by President Grant to be Secretary of the Treasury, arrived at the Grand Union Hotel in Saratoga Springs, New York for his usual summer stay there. The embarrassed manager refused to allow him to register, saying that the owner, Henry Hilton (no relation to the more famous Conrad Hilton), decided that Jews were bad for business. Hilton himself, the model of WASP rectitude, was involved in bribery and graft through his participation in the Tweed Ring. But I digress.

Seligman and his friends were shocked, but Hilton refused to budge. This started the pattern of excluding Jews from different areas of upper-crust society. Jews, who had been founders of various Union League Clubs throughout the country, discovered that their own children were refused membership. Jews were forced to start their own clubs and hotels to compensate for the WASP snubs. The Jewish clubs were almost always better and fancier than the WASP ones, but the sense of inferiority remained.

What about Henry Hilton, who started all this? Well, sometimes, we do get revenge. Hilton had been the head of a dry-goods chain called the A.T. Stewart Company. Most of the Stewart customers were Jews, who boycotted the company, destroying it – and Hilton.

Violent Anti-Semitism

This social anti-Semitism, however, didn't touch the immigrant masses. They were used to anti-Semitism in a cruder form: Violent. That form of Jew-hate was less popular in America than in Europe. There were two major exceptions to that rule.

In 1902, as we mentioned earlier, 100,000 Jews attended the funeral of Rabbi Jacob Joseph. The procession passed the factory of the R. Hoe Company, whose workers were mostly Irish. They thought it would be great fun to throw heavy metal objects at the solemn Jewish mourners below (obviously anticipating the Intifada rock-throwers). After several mourners had been badly injured, the crowd tried to fight back. Then the police arrived.

Anyone who has ever lived in a city can guess what nationality the police were. The cops were shocked that their compatriots at the R. Hoe Company were being threatened by those rabble-rousing Jews. They began beating as many of the mourners as they could, leaving dozens more Jews injured. Mayor Seth Low called for an investigation, and various heads rolled, but the immigrants felt that even in America a pogrom was possible.

The second incident of violence is far more famous, having been turned into a TV movie. In 1913 Atlanta, a young girl named Mary Phagan was found murdered in a pencil factory where she worked. The factory's manager was a Jew named Leo Frank. Although from New York, Frank had quickly become an established figure in the Atlanta Jewish community through his involvement in Bnai Brith and other communal groups.

Frank was one of two suspects in the murder; the other was a black man who had worked in the factory. The prosecutors, who were not stupid, despite being Deep South bigots, knew that the worker had committed the murder, but focused their efforts on Frank anyway. Why? Because in those days, getting a conviction against a black man was so typical as to be boring. But a northern Jewboy, ah, that would be quite an achievement.

And so it went. A white-trash jury convicted Frank as the shouts of "Kill the Jew" rang out around the courthouse (sort of like the Dreyfus trial, but the racists weren't as rude). Eventually, Georgia Governor John Slaton, refusing to let an innocent man be executed, commuted Frank's death sentence. For that act, Slaton ended his promising political career. Although he was played by Jack Lemmon in the movie, the real Slaton was closer in age to Lemmon's actor son, Chris; so Slaton destroyed what would have been a long political career.

The unfortunate Frank wasn't off the hook. A mob found out where he was imprisoned, kidnapped him, and lynched him. There exists a photo of the lynching party: Frank's body is hanging from a tree, and the members of the mob are milling around, proud of their noble act of revenge. The children and grandchildren of this mob eventually grew up to attack civil rights workers in the '60s. However, we hope that their great-grandchildren have joined the human race.

The Frank incident sent shockwaves throughout the Southern Jewish community. Many Jews fled the South or at least sent their children away. Even today, older Jews from the area remember the fear that emanated from the affair. As for the bad guys in this whole matter, like the prosecutors, the anti-Semitic agitators, etc., they all became very successful in Georgia politics, proving, once again, that anti-Semitism pays.

Economic Anti-Semitism

For all the fear and terror that the Frank affair spread among Jews of the South, the immigrant masses were not that affected by it. For most of them, the South might as well have been a foreign country (which, in many ways, it was). They were concerned about anti-Semitism that hit them directly, and that took the form of economic anti-Semitism.

In the 1920s, 90% of all classified ads for white-collar positions were for Christians only. The result of that was that Jews couldn't find jobs working for established companies, and that you found a lot of Jews named Cohen who suddenly had new last names like Cowan and Conn.

In fields like medicine and law, Jews had hard times as well. Jewish med school graduates had nowhere to become interns, as the local hospitals refused to hire them. That's one of the reasons we have all those "Jewish" hospitals today. They were set up as places for Jewish doctors to practice. Today, the purpose behind these hospitals has long since disappeared, but local Jewish federations keep funding them, to the detriment of more important Jewish concerns, like education.

As for law, WASP firms refused to hire Jewish associates (or many Catholic ones as well). Jews were forced to form their own firms, or go into fields that the WASP firms neglected, such as personal injury, bankruptcy, and criminal law. To the WASPs' dismay, Jews quickly came to dominate those fields, and some did quite well financially. Today, many of those stridently anti-Semitic firms even have Orthodox Jewish partners and associates.

In business, Jews, unable to get jobs working for non-Jewish companies, were forced to become risk-taking entrepreneurs. Yet with risk comes the possibility of reward, and many of these Jewish businessmen became very successful. However, Dun & Bradstreet had declared Jews to be bad credit risks, and few, if any, banks would lend them money. So where did Jewish businessmen get their initial capital? From internal sources within the community. The immigrants founded thousands of loan societies, mutual benefit societies, and credit unions, all of which financed Jewish enterprises. In addition, less formal loans from relatives played a key part. Once a business started operating, many owners would load the payroll with family members, further helping the community. This was the case in even the most successful companies. Movie mogul Louis B. Mayer put so many family members on his payroll that someone said that MGM stood for "Mayer's Gantse Mishpoche [Mayer's whole family]."

Educational Anti-Semitism

To the immigrant generation, education was the ticket for upward mobility for their children. By 1919, 9.7% of the students in professional schools in the United States were Jewish, three times the population percentage. As for colleges, City College was 85% Jewish; NYU – 21%; Columbia – 40%; and Harvard – 15%.

In the 60s, college was a place for protesting the evils of the world; in the 80s, college was a place to learn how to make a lot of money. In the teens and 20s, college was a place where young WASP males bonded together by having a good time, and working just hard enough to get "Gentlemen's Cs" for their courses.

Into this comfortable world came the Jewish student: He (and sometimes she) was hard-working and serious. Too serious. The Jews were always studying, and not having fun. They were messing up the curve. They were ruining the atmosphere of good old Ivy U. These arguments should sound familiar: They are usually raised today about Oriental students. And just as some administrators are trying to institute a quota for Oriental students, colleges tried to do that to Jewish students in the 1920s.

The anti-Jewish quotas were very successful. Columbia, for example, dropped its Jewish population from 40% to 22% in only three years, causing Hazzan Gershom Seixas, who had been a Columbia trustee for 30 years (1786-1816), to take a few spins in his grave.

The big battle over quotas, however, was at Harvard. Then, as now, Harvard had the big name. The new president of Harvard, A. Lawrence Lowell, was fiercely anti-Semitic, and wanted to cut down the number of Jews at his school.[1] This time the Jews fought back. They were assisted by Lowell's predecessor, Charles Eliot, a man who believed in merit, rather than racism. By this time, there were also a number of Jewish alumni,

---

1.   Lowell also proved the rule that anyone with an initial for a first name is inherently dangerous (or have you forgotten J. Edgar Hoover, J. William Fulbright, G. Gordon Liddy, and a host of others?)

who fought against the imposition of quotas. Julian Mack was on the Harvard Board of Trustees, and rallied his associates against Lowell.

The Jews' most interesting allies were the Irish of Cambridge. They had always resented Harvard's snobby behavior towards them. The local Irish politicos, seeing an opportunity to strike back at that disliked institution, told Harvard that they would review its tax-exempt status in light of its prejudiced policies.

Finally, the Harvard faculty voted on the issue, and the quotas were defeated – or were they? In only a few years, the Jewish percentage at Harvard dropped into single digits. The anti-quota forces forgot that setting policy is one matter; implementing it is another. Lowell instructed his allies in the admissions office to take "geographical" and other factors into account – factors that would cut down the Jewish percentage (after all, not many Jews, if you're recruiting students from Montana).

An interesting flip-side to the geographical quota issue was the desire of schools located in areas with few Jews to actively pursue Jewish students. For example, University of South Carolina wanted to increase its Jewish enrollment, but got no takers. First, few Jews could afford to go to college so far from home; second, most Jewish freshmen wanted to go to school in an area where there would be a decent number of Jews.

The quota system went out of business after World War Two, to be replaced by merit until affirmative action arrived on the scene in the late 60s. Today, Harvard is about 25% Jewish; Columbia – 40%; Princeton – 20%. Percentages at the law and medical schools at major universities are even higher. Many of the institutions that were among the worse offenders in the quota department have had Jewish presidents in recent years. In 1945, Dartmouth President Ernest Hopkins declared that his institution "is a Christian college funded for the Christianization of its students." Since then, Dartmouth has had two Jewish presidents. Is this a great country or what? One major university stood firm against quotas, and therefore always had many Jewish students: The University of Chicago (my law school alma mater). It is not surprising that U of C leads the nation's universities in Nobel Prize winners.

There will always be a high percentage of Jewish students wherever merit rules over quotas. Just as the Jewish numbers at the Ivies has gone up, City College shows what happens if Jews flee a school. If you tell any young New Yorker that City College was once one of the finest colleges in the country, he'd think you were about to try to sell him a bridge in Brooklyn. But it's true. However, when the City University made the decision that quality and merit would no longer be factors at City College, the Jewish students left en masse. The result is an institution not much better than a community college.

Memories of the quotas died hard. That's why Jews are so opposed to affirmative action. One of the best lines regarding the quota system was said by the famous American Jewish leader, Rabbi Stephen Wise. He was speaking at the dedication of the Princeton Hillel House in the late 40s, shortly before his death. Princeton was then known as the Ivy most unfriendly towards Jews, but Wise was still expected to say the usual platitudes about how nice Princeton was, etc., etc. Instead, Wise began his speech by saying, "How nice it is that Princeton has finally let in enough Jews to establish a Hillel house."[1]

Anti-Immigration Anti-Semitism

For years, Congress had been trying to pass anti-immigration legislation. Three groups were especially forceful against immigration:

1) The hicks in the sticks. They viewed the cities as the source of all evil, as opposed to the wholesome life of rural America (you can almost hear the "Andy Griffith" theme music in the background). The fewer immigrants, the less evil.

---

1. Change comes everywhere. In 1971, Princeton established one of the few kosher dining facilities run directly by the university. In 1985, it re-scheduled the first day of classes to prevent a conflict with Rosh Hashana.

2) The old WASP elite. This group, led by people with names like Cabot
    and Lowell and Adams and Lodge, thought that immigration was okay
    – if the immigrants came from England or Scandinavia, not from
    Russia or Italy. The latter were a lower breed of person, polluting and
    diluting good old-fashioned WASP America.

3) The American labor movement (except for the Jewish unions) wanted
    to see an end to the continual inflow of cheap labor. If immigration
    would énd, union wages, buoyed by a smaller workforce, could rise.

The early anti-immigration laws first proposed a literacy test. Jewish
groups got that law amended to include literacy in any language (virtually
all the immigrants could read Hebrew). But in 1924, the battle was lost.
The Johnson Act closed America's doors to the Jews of Eastern Europe by
imposing a stringent quota on immigrants from that area.

For many, if not most, anti-immigration advocates, Jews were not the
main target: The nativists wanted to keep out Catholics, especially Italians
and Slavs. But the Johnson Act affected the Jews far more than any other
ethnic group. First, it locked the Jewish population in place until the end
of the 1940s. For the first time since the 1820s, immigration would be a
negligible factor in American Jewish life. Secondly, the Johnson Act led to
the deaths of tens of thousands of Jews who would have escaped the
Holocaust to America, but more about that later.

Henry Ford Anti-Semitism

Old Henry gets his own chapter in the history of American anti-Semitism,
having caused more damage than most other individuals. In 1920, Ford
began running a serialized version of "The Protocols of the Elders of Zion"
in his newspaper, the Dearborn Independent.

"Protocols" is purportedly an account of the secret Jewish plan to rule
the world. It was written by a Russian official as part of the Czar's anti-
Jewish policy. "Protocols" was to justify the Russian anti-Semitic policy
by showing how dangerous the Jews were. Anyone who knows anything

about Jews would realize how farfetched "Protocols" is. Jewish leaders are supposedly united in trying to take over the world. If Jewish leaders ever got together to plan anything important, they'd be at each others' throats within ten minutes arguing about "Who is a Jew," "Orthodox vs. Conservative vs. Reform," "Land for Peace," etc.

Ford, a strange duck to begin with, apparently thought "Protocols" presented the Gospel truth (to coin a phrase). After he began the book's publication, a large committee of American VIPs asked him to stop. This committee included people like former President William (the "Refrigerator") Taft, not known for being friendly towards Jews. Ford was not moved.

It took two things to finally get Ford to end publication of "Protocols." First was a national Jewish-led boycott of Ford cars. Second was a lawsuit by a Detroit Jewish lawyer named Aaron Sapiro. Sapiro had been accused of fraud by the Independent. The lawyer sued Ford for libel. The car maker avoided service of process and stalled the trial as long as possible, but was finally on the verge of getting hit with a large judgment. At that point, Ford caved in. The pocketbook talks even when common sense doesn't. Ford settled with Sapiro and agreed to apologize for publishing "Protocols." Big deal; the damage was done. Ford had been spreading his anti-Semitic poison for seven years while the boycott and lawsuit were going on.

Ironically, "Protocols" would find a receptive audience in the Dearborn, Michigan of today. Dearborn has become the Palestinian center of the United States. These new Dearborners have such a hate for Israel and Jews that they'd probably think "Protocols" was an understatement of the facts. Incidentally, for years, copies of "Protocols" were given out by King Fahd of Saudi Arabia and his predecessors as evidence of Israel's plot to take over the world. The Saudis may still be doing this for all we know.

The spread of "Protocols" hit me a few years ago. I was in the Chicago Public Library's main branch, when I saw a neat stack of a dozen brand-new copies of "Protocols" on the shelf. I thought that this was an examination of "Protocols" on the level of Norman Cohn's classic analysis,

"Warrant for Genocide." But no-o-o-o-o! These were copies of the classic "Protocols," presented as a straight work of non-fiction, and published by a Holocaust revisionist institute out West. Apparently, someone on the staff of the Chicago Public Library thinks that "Protocols" is a true story. I was so disgusted that my tax dollars were being spent to buy anti-Semitic propaganda that I promptly moved to Skokie.

Depression Anti-Semitism

Tough economic times lead to a search for a scapegoat, and guess who that usually is. That's the European model of anti-Semitism. Fortunately, the Depression in America was not as bad as it could have been, and led to "only" three new forms of anti-Semitism:

1) Father Charles Coughlin. The Michigan Catholic priest had a national radio show in which he accused Jews of everything short of poisoning the wells. Church leaders said that they couldn't silence Coughlin because their hands were tied by the First Amendment. When federal agents began checking into the revocation of the Church's tax-exempt status, the Church's hands got untied pretty darn fast.

2) Nazi sympathizers. A German named Fritz Kuhn led an organization called the Bund, a group of would-be Nazis. When they tried to cause trouble for Jews in the cities, Jewish gangs would bust their heads. That tended to reduce their enthusiasm for Jew-baiting. Once WWII began, the Bund was regarded as an enemy organization and wasn't heard from again.

3) Isolationists. These good folks from America's midwestern heartland believed that a Jewish conspiracy was out to get the U.S. involved in the War in Europe. They were led by national hero and ignoramus Charles Lindbergh, whose anti-Semitism was so strident that he drove away most of the honest isolationists. As with the Bund, WWII put an end to their trouble-making.

Ironically, it was the Nazi Kristallnacht pogrom in 1938 that dampened some of the open anti-Semitic feeling in America. People saw what prejudice could lead to, and sympathy for the Jews increased. Sympathy for Jews always escalates when we're getting killed or attacked. That's why Israel is the world's number one villain; it's not playing the game by the old rules. Now, if Israel could just lose a war, its popularity would be tremendous.

FDR – King of the Jews

Franklin Roosevelt was the great hero of the Jews, and not until his non-role in the Holocaust was revealed in the late 60s, did he lose that title. To quote Judge Jonah Goldstein, Jews had three "velts" (worlds): Die velt (this world), yenne velt (the world to come), and Roosevelt. Domestically speaking, FDR deserves the accolades. He had many Jewish advisers from his days as New York governor, who helped set up the New Deal after Roosevelt's election. Despite attacks on his program as the "Jew Deal," Roosevelt stood by his policies and his advisors.

The New Deal provided work for Jewish artists (on WPA projects), economists, architects, and other professionals. But the Jews who benefited the most were the lawyers. Closed out of the WASP law firms, they entered the federal government in droves. It was Jewish lawyers who established the various New Deal agencies, and set up their rules and regulations. After WWII, it was those same lawyers who were called to private practice to interpret the rules they had written a decade earlier. The law firms who hired these lawyers might not have liked Jews, but they sure needed them.

Jews rewarded Roosevelt with over 90% of their vote every four years. Roosevelt's election also led to the rise of other Jewish politicians: New York Governor Herbert Lehman, Illinois Governor Henry Horner, and Treasury Secretary Henry Morgenthau. In the House of Representatives, Emanuel Celler, Sol Bloom, and Adolph Sabath rose to powerful positions. But more about these folks later.

Henry Horner's election as the first Jewish governor of Illinois came in a state with a much smaller Jewish population than that of New York. In fact, outside Cook County (Chicago), there were few Jews. Horner's real name was Henry Levy. When he was an infant, his parents divorced. A distraught Mrs. Levy went home to her mother, Mrs. Horner. Grandma Horner agreed to let her daughter move back home only if she changed her three sons' last names to Horner. Mrs. Levy compromised with her mother: The two older boys would keep the name Levy; infant Henry would change his last name to Horner.

Flash forward to 1932, where Probate Judge Horner, the Democratic candidate for governor, has called a meeting of all 102 Illinois Democratic County Chairmen. He said, "Boys, I have something to tell you. My name was originally Henry Levy." Horner told them the story of his name change. "I wanted you all to know the truth in case the Republicans started spreading any stories about me."

The cigar-chomping chairmen nodded. "Sure, Judge. We'll make sure the people hear the truth."

The chairmen went back to their respective counties throughout Illinois, and called together their troops. "Boys. Judge Horner's real name was Henry Levy." A gasp of fear from the party workers. "But he changed it to Henry Horner – when he converted to Christianity." Horner won in a landslide.

CHAPTER 6

AMERICA AND THE HOLOCAUST

We now come to a very sensitive issue in American Jewish history: The Holocaust. Did the Jews do enough? What else should they have done? Who were the heroes? Who were the villains? Don't worry. I'll answer all those questions. In the interests of full disclosure, however, I must state my own background. During the Holocaust, my parents were living in and escaping from ghettos in Poland, just barely staying alive, while American Jews were kvetching about gas rationing and nylon shortages. But I shall be as objective as I can.

In 1933, when Hitler took over in Germany, American Jews became very alarmed.[1] Many Jews wanted to organize a boycott of German goods; other Jews thought that a boycott would work against the German Jews, and preferred quiet diplomacy. A boycott was begun despite the disagreement. Was the boycott effective? We have since learned that the boycott was **very** effective against Germany from an economic perspective. Germany was trying desperately to export goods, and the American Jews were choking them.

---

1. Non-Jewish Americans, on the other hand, did not take Hitler seriously because he looked like a cross between Charlie Chaplin and Moe Howard.

On the other hand, the boycott did nothing to dissuade the Germans from their anti-Semitic course. We're talking about a people who would gladly eliminate their greatest scientists and artists in the name of ethnic purity; a people who would later be willing to divert badly needed troop supply trains to transport Jews to Auschwitz. A boycott might have dissuaded a normal nation, not the dysfunctional Deutschland.

As everybody knows, things just got worse and worse for the German Jews throughout the 30s, climaxing in the Kristallnacht pogrom of November, 1938. The Jews were desperate to get out – anywhere. But no country was willing to accept them, especially the Land of the Free, Home of the Brave.

The U.S. guilt regarding the failure to rescue the Jews of Europe first emerged as a public issue in 1967, with the publication of Arthur Morse's "While Six Million Died." In that book, FDR, hero of the Jews, emerges as an uncaring patrician, uninterested in the fate of the European Jews and unwilling to lift a finger to help them. The U.S. had replaced Emma Lazarus's poem on the Statue of Liberty ("Give me your tired, your poor...") with a sign reading "Go Away!"

How guilty was Roosevelt? In the 1930s, anti-immigration sentiment was extremely strong in the United States, fueled by the Depression. Of course, part of that sentiment was related to the nature of the immigrants. In 1939, New York Senator Robert Wagner tried to pass a bill to admit 20,000 Jewish kids into the U.S. The bill got nowhere. Undaunted, Wagner said, how about if we keep those kids in Alaska instead of the continental U.S.? No way, said Congress. A year later, when it was proposed that British kids be allowed into the U.S. during the Battle of Britain, Congress said, Sure, send us all you want.

Roosevelt could take the pulse of public opinion as well as any politician. He simply didn't want to expend his political capital on an issue that so many people were against. In that respect, he was a mere politician, not Roosevelt the statesman of American history.

Roosevelt's main guilt comes from not doing the little things that he could have gotten away with. In 1938, the S.S. St. Louis had sailed from Germany, filled with refugees who thought they had passes to enter the Dominican Republic. But when the passengers got to that island, they discovered that their passes were invalid. Where to now? They were right off the coast of Miami, but the U.S. would not let the refugees enter. In such a situation, the government could have interned the refugees, stating that the ship was about to sink, or some other bogus story. But the U.S. stuck to its guns, and the St. Louis was sent back to Europe. The whole affair became the movie, "Voyage of the Damned."

Another of Roosevelt's failures was his refusal to put any pressure on England to open the doors of Palestine. He said he didn't want to get involved in another country's internal affairs. Gimme a break! We weren't asking the Brits to abolish the monarchy or to drive on the right side of the road; all the Jews wanted was for England to abide by the Balfour Declaration. In fact, Roosevelt had plenty of leverage over England. Britain needed all the aid it could get from the U.S.; if FDR had said, Open the damn doors, they'd have been opened.

One problem was that the patrician FDR really didn't like Jews as much as his admirers and detractors assumed. At one point, he told Interior Secretary Harold Ickes that he agreed with Joseph Kennedy that Jews had too much control over the American government. Does that sound like someone who would put himself out to help European Jewry?

The result of all this was that German Propaganda Minister Goebbels sang to Hitler, "The Hindus hate the Moslems, and the Moslems hate the Hindus, the Protestants hate the Catholics, and everybody hates the Jews." Despite Goebbels' failure to properly credit Tom Lehrer for that song, he was correct. The world's refusal to help the Jews, especially the American apathy, convinced the Nazis that they could go ahead with the Final Solution with no interference.

Amazingly, during the War itself, the quotas for immigrants from countries the Jews were escaping remained unfilled. Why is that? In short, because Jews have always had bad luck. Historically, the State Department has been a haven of anti-Semitism throughout American history.[1] The Assistant Secretary of State for Refugee Affairs during these critical times, however, was a Jew-hater even by State Department standards. Breckenridge Long issued orders that every picayune regulation and rule should be invoked to prevent any Jews from entering the United States. Long was quite successful; he was personally responsible for the deaths of hundreds, if not thousands, of Jews.

After Long's death, his diaries were published. It turns out that not only was Long an anti-Semite, but he was a psychopath as well. Based on statements written in his diaries, Long should have been in a hospital for the criminally insane; and this was the man upon whose shoulders the fate of hundreds of Jews rested. That Holy-One-Blessed-Be-He, what a sense of humor.

By 1942, reports were coming out of Europe detailing the Final Solution, but the State Department suppressed all such reports. Within a year, however, the news had leaked out. Even the Yeshiva University student newspaper, the Commentator, published stories about the murder of the Jews.

Finally, in 1944, Treasury Secretary Morgenthau managed to get Long ousted. Roosevelt allowed Morgenthau and his bright young assistants (who weren't Jewish, but were caring humanitarians) to set up the War Refugee Board, to help the Jews of Europe. Just one problem: There weren't many European Jews left to save. Hungary was the sight of the only major pocket of living Jews. The War Refugee Board did what it could, especially in pumping money and aid to the great Raul Wallenberg, who saved hundreds of lives. But for the most part, the War Refugee Board was too little, too late.

There was one final chance for the U.S. to save Jewish lives. American bombers were flying right over Auschwitz, where trains were arriving daily, with thousands of victims. If the train lines could be blown up, it would throw a money wrench in the Germans' operation.

---

1.   And you thought James Baker wasn't a traditionalist.

The decision was rendered by the man in charge, John J. McCloy: No! Bombing Auschwitz would take away from the war effort (though the planes flew right over the camp anyway). In addition, the Germans will retaliate against American POWs (Huh?). Maybe McCloy sincerely believed these explanations. How can we tell? As with General Grant, let's examine McCloy's post-War activities.

McCloy was appointed High Commissioner for Germany. In that position, he took a forgive-and-forget policy towards the former Nazis, allowing ex-killers to resume holding positions of power and responsibility. He then returned to New York and his old-line law firm, which he kept closed to Jews as long as possible. Do you see a pattern here?

Based on his Auschwitz decision, McCloy is probably responsible for the deaths of more Jews than any other single American (this probably upsets Breckenridge Long, but he's a distant second). In 1982, to commemorate his 90th birthday,[1] McCloy received the Medal of Freedom from President Reagan. The ceremony was probably arranged by the same geniuses who set up Reagan's visit to the SS graves at Bitburg.

Now, with this depressing background behind us, we can ask the big question: Could American Jews have helped more? Answer: Not really, for three reasons.

1) The Jews were very divided. Earlier in the century, the Jewish community knew who its leader was: Louis Marshall. People (especially Zionists) disagreed with him, but he was still regarded as the community's Numero Uno. Marshall died in 1929, and was not replaced. Zionists fought with non-Zionists; Orthodox with non- Orthodox; unionists with business-owners. Even Roosevelt said he wished the Jews had a pope, so he would know who to deal with. Long, on the other hand, wrote gleefully of Jewish disunity in his diary.

2) Bad leadership in government. Eventually, Secretary Morgenthau and Congressman Celler refused to take any more State Department crap,

---

1. Anti-Semites tend to have long lives. A study is underway to determine if hatred of Jews reduces the level of LDL cholesterol (that is, the bad cholesterol).

and stood up for their fellow Jews. Powerful congressmen Sol Bloom of New York and Adolph Sabath of Chicago were another story. They said and did nothing for 12 years. It wasn't really their fault. Most men have a sac of thin skin between their legs, containing two almond- shaped organs; unfortunately, Bloom and Sabath didn't.

If the two ever said anything to FDR about the Jews, the conversation probably went like this:

Bloom: Mr. President. Will you do anything to save the Jews?

FDR: No, Sol. Not a damn thing, The polls show the people are against it.

Bloom: Oh, thank you, Mr. President.

Contrast this with Jacob Schiff in 1911. President Taft held a meeting with Jewish leaders, at which time he refused their request to break a treaty with Russia over its anti-Semitism. When the meeting ended, Taft put out his hand to Schiff. Schiff refused to shake the President's hand, gave him a dirty look, and stalked out. At least Schiff let the President know where he stood.

In his best-seller, "Chutzpah," Alan Dershowitz is especially hard on Felix Frankfurter. The Supreme Court Justice had been one of FDR's closest advisors, but said nothing before, during, or after the Holocaust, which Dershowitz finds inexcusable. He hopes that if he is ever in Frankfurter's position, he, Dershowitz, will speak out for his fellow Jews. It is this hope that causes Dershowitz and others to speak out on Israel's behalf, even if some find their efforts a tad strident.[1]

3) Jewish influence on American foreign policy is limited. This is a very scary thought, but true. We can't push U.S. foreign policy where it doesn't

---

1. If anything, Dershowitz went easy on Frankfurter. While he aided Brandeis in Zionist matters in the 1910s, after 1921, Frankfurter had nothing to do with the Jewish community, and had no relationship with Jewish friends from his childhood. In 1940, Frankfurter adopted two non-Jewish British Blitz orphans. Two years later, he refused to believe courageous Polish emissary Jan Karski, who was one of the earliest sources of news of the Final Solution. Between Frankfurter and Dershowitz, I'll take Dershowitz any day.

want to go, especially if the president and State Department are unfriendly. We saw that in 1956 after the Sinai Campaign, when John Foster ("Sour-Pickle Face") Dulles threatened a cut-off of Israel Bond money if Ben-Gurion didn't order a pull-out from Sinai. More recently, we saw President Bush refuse Israel's loan guarantee request, and declare that he was "one lonely man" standing against the nefarious forces of the evil Israel lobby.

Despite the fact that the Jews would probably not have made a difference in WWII, they still should have made their voices heard more strongly. Who knows? Maybe something would have happened. Maybe FDR would have ordered Auschwitz bombed if he knew that his buddies, allies, advisors, and supporters were so mad. But that's all "maybe" and "what if."

The failure to do anything to save the Jews of Europe led to strong guilt feelings among American Jews. These feelings would be translated into action; first, for Israel, and then for Soviet Jewry.

Post-Holocaust Refugees: My Parents Come to America

After the War's end, about 140,000 Holocaust refugees made their way to the United States, the most important of whom were my mother (1946) and father (1949).[1] This was the first major Jewish immigration since the early 20s. You would assume that after the enormity of the Holocaust became known, Congress, full of guilt over its inaction during the 30s, would open the doors wide for the refugees. Well, you'd be wrong.

Congress was still filled with reactionaries who shuddered at the thought of any more Jews being let into WASP America. With quotas still in place, though partially modified, the 150,000 Jews trickled into the States over the period of about six years. Some Jews in Europe, learning of the restrictive situation from American relatives, were smart enough to change their identification documents to reflect a birthplace in

---

1. "Importance" is all a matter of perspective, don't you think?

Germany rather than Poland (the German quota would take much longer to fill).

But let it not be said that Congress was without humanity or sentiment. In passing new immigration laws, Congress agreed to enlarge the quotas allocated to the Eastern European countries – but with the condition that the extra places be reserved for non-Jewish "refugees from Communism." Many, if not most, of these non-Jewish refugees were war criminals who had assisted the Nazis in killing Jews. You can be damn sure **they** didn't want to face the Communists.

Thus, hundreds of war criminals were admitted into the United States, to live out their years in comfort and security. Beginning in the 1970s, a few of these killers were discovered, but the vast majority were not. Here's an example: I knew non-Jews who lived in Chicago's Marquette Park neighborhood. They told me that there were many older folks living there who had come over as refugees from Lithuania after the War. These people kept to themselves, spoke little English, and never ever said a word about their wartime experiences. Yet, it was assumed among other people in the neighborhood, none of whom were Jewish, that these aging Lithuanians were hiding criminal backgrounds. No one from Marquette Park has ever been charged with any war crimes, so maybe the neighbors are all imagining things. Then again, over 90% of Lithuanian Jewry was murdered with the active assistance of the general Lithuanian population, so maybe it's **not** their imagination.

I know I'll hear anguished protests from Lithuanians over the previous paragraph, so let me say the magic words: "Many Lithuanians risked their lives to hide and save Jews during the Holocaust." There – stop your kvetching and complaining.

As for the Jewish refugees, they weren't concerned about the war criminals. They were only interested in re-building their lives. The vast majority of them succeeded, and became the latest examples of the American Dream. However, it took many years until discussion of their wartime experiences would become a mainstream topic. That will be discussed in greater detail later.

CHAPTER 7

THE BIRTH OF ISRAEL: AMERICAN JEWS FIND A CAUSE

American Jews channeled their guilt feelings over the Holocaust into energy and support for the efforts to establish a Jewish state in Palestine. Leadership of the American Zionist movement had shifted from Stephen Wise to the imperious Cleveland rabbi, Abba Hillel Silver.[1]

By 1947, the Zionist efforts were concentrated in getting U.S. and other world support for the United Nations partition plan, which would divide Palestine into two states, one Jewish and one Arab.[2] Another Zionist activity was the smuggling of arms from the U.S. to the Hagana. Various Jewish mobsters contributed to that effort, and J. Edgar Hoover agreed to turn a blind eye to the gun-running operation, if it could be kept quiet.

On November 29, 1947, the U.N. passed the partition plan. Celebrations erupted in the streets of Jewish neighborhoods throughout the country, but Silver and other Zionist leaders knew the hard battles were still ahead. The next step was to lobby President Truman to grant

---

1. It sure takes a lot of chutzpah to be imperious if you come from Cleveland.
2. The Arabs weren't opposed to the existence of an independent Jewish state; they just wanted it to be located at a point midway between the Tel-Aviv and Cyprus coasts.

the Jewish state recognition when it officially proclaimed its independence. That wouldn't be easy; the State Department (yes, them again) was adamantly pro-Arab. Also, Truman hated Silver, whose aggressive, take-no-prisoners lobbying style rubbed him the wrong way.

The Zionists had powerful allies in Truman's advisor, Clark Clifford, and in the president's former business partner, Eddie Jacobson, who arranged a meeting of Truman and Chaim Weizmann. The old Zionist leader impressed the president, who eventually rejected the Arabists, and recognized Israel.

Truman's role in all this has been exaggerated. It is true that he overcame his youthful aversion to Jews, and that he swiftly recognized Israel, but that was about it. No aid, no arms sales, not even a good old-fashioned Truman pep talk. However, look at the alternative: FDR. Shortly before he died, Roosevelt had a meeting with King Saud of Saudi Arabia (a name not unlike "Jim Brown of the Cleveland Browns"). Roosevelt emerged from that meeting stating that he had learned more about the Near East[1] in just a short meeting with Saud than he had in longer discussions with other people. Guess who "other people" are: People like Frankfurter, Morgenthau, Celler, etc.

Thankfully, Roosevelt died when he did. Had he been president during the crucial period in 1947-48, he would have listened to the State Department, and the partition plan would have never passed. Does this sound mean-spirited? Well, it's a tough world out there.

The American Jewish community was already the most charity-giving group in the country. However, swept up in its enthusiasm, the Jews broke all earlier records in raising money for Israel. The United Jewish Appeal raised a record $150 million in 1947. The next year, the UJA brought in $200 million.

But money wasn't the only thing sent to Israel. Several thousand young Americans fought there as volunteers. The most famous of them was Colonel David "Mickey" Marcus. Marcus was a West Point graduate, who,

---

1. The region later moved next door, and became the "Middle East."

being a good Jewish boy, left the Army for law school, becoming a prosecutor in New York. He returned to the Army to serve with distinction in WWII. In Israel, Marcus became the overall commander of the Jerusalem front, the first Jewish general in the ancestral homeland since Simon Bar-Cochba 1,812 years earlier. Marcus successfully built the "Burma Road," which kept Jerusalem supplied while under Arab siege.

Then, tragedy struck. One night, Mickey left his tent, wrapped in a white sheet, to urinate behind the bushes. When he returned, the sentry, a new immigrant who knew no English, told him to halt. Mickey, who knew little Hebrew, kept going. The sentry fired at the scary white sheet, and Marcus was killed.[1] In Israel, streets were named for him; in the Bronx, he was honored with the "David Marcus" movie theater. The rest of America learned about Marcus in the 1968 movie, "Cast a Giant Shadow," with Kirk Douglas as Mickey. In real life (as opposed to reel life), Mickey had no cleft in his chin, and was balding and pudgy, with a powerful look about him.

When the war ended, most of the American volunteers returned home. As the years went on, the glory of the struggle for independence was replaced by the prosaic activity of building a country with little money, and filled with immigrants from throughout the world. Israel was placed on the back burner in the American Jewish mindset.

In 1956, Israel once again occupied the American Jewish scene, after its invasion of the Sinai peninsula, following years of terrorist attacks from there. Eisenhower and Dulles, the 50s version of Bush and Baker, put the screws on Israel to withdraw, and it reluctantly did so. However, the U.N. placed a military force of its own in Sinai, and Egypt was prevented from stationing any troops there. Israel was able to rest easy, knowing it had the backing of the nations of the world. [Insert sarcastic smirk here.] Once again, Israel was placed in the American Jewish background, to return for good in 1967.

---

1. The only case in history where not paying enough attention in Hebrew school proved fatal.

CHAPTER 8

AMERICAN JEWISH HISTORY: THE PAST 50 YEARS

We now enter a period of history that many of us know first-hand. If I try to review it all, I'll just get letters saying, "You forgot this" or "You left that out." That's why there's a bibliography. Therefore, rather than re-hash it all, I'd like to take an overview[1] of a few selected topics:

1. The Decline of Anti-Semitism

In the late 1940s, anti-Semitism was still powerful in the United States. A 1944 poll revealed that one-third of those asked would be sympathetic to an anti-Semitic political campaign. Even in 1948, when the truth of the Holocaust was known to all, 60% of Americans wanted to limit the influx of Jewish Displaced Persons.

Then, as if the country had lanced a huge poisonous boil, anti-Semitism popped, and began to dissipate in the early 1950s. Barriers against Jews began falling in the worlds of commerce and education (no more quotas

---

1. "Take an overview" is either New Yorkese like "take a haircut" or Hollywoodese like "take a meeting."

and no affirmative action yet). WASP law firms admitted Jewish partners; hospitals granted Jewish doctors admitting privileges; and corporations hired Jewish executives. Who'd have imagined that the head of one of America's oldest companies, duPont, would be named Irving Shapiro?

All this did not mean that Jews were secure – memories of Coughlin and quotas ran deep – but to the pleasant surprise of most Jews, various incidents that, in the past, would have led to a rise in anti-Semitism, hardly registered in the national consciousness.

First, the Rosenberg trial. Would all Jews be viewed as traitors? No. The Rosenbergs' Benedict Arnold act did not lead to a significant rise in anti-Jewish attitudes. Perhaps that was because virtually everyone involved in the trial, from the judge on down, was Jewish too.

Next, Joe McCarthy's witchhunts. Unlike the post-WWI anti-Communist hysteria, the 1950s version did not unduly target Jews. In fact, McCarthy's main targets were upper-class WASPs, and his chief advisor was Roy Cohn. McCarthy was attacked by noted anti-Semite Gerald L.K. Smith for failing to show the "obvious" ties between Jews and Communism.

A generation later, in 1973, Jews again "tzittered" (shivered) when the Arabs instituted the oil boycott against the U.S. for supporting Israel in the Yom Kippur War. Would Jews get the blame for gas shortages and rising prices? Again, the answer was no. Of course, many Jewish groups looked under every rock in the Ozarks for anti-Semites, and usually found some, but in America, crackpots are in the fringe, not the mainstream.

Finally, the 1980s saw the Wall Street insider trading scandals – starring a cast of, mostly, Jews, – and the Jonathan Pollard spy mess. Neither raised anti-Semitic attitudes. In fact, polls showed that of those Americans who even heard of Pollard, most had no idea for whom he had spied.

America today is probably the least anti-Jewish nation in the history of the Diaspora. That doesn't mean that the U.S. lacks its fair share of right-wing crazies in Idaho and Arizona, as well as left-wing loonies on major college campuses. However, most Americans are not secretly planning pogroms on Easter Sunday. Maybe my standards are lower than those of the organized Jewish defense groups. I don't expect Christians to love Jews, or even to like Jews; if they don't actively dislike us or hate us, I'm satisfied. In any event, most non-Jews have no time to hate us; they're too busy marrying us (more on that later).

2. The Suburbanized Jewish Community

As the Jews started rising in affluence, they pursued the most solid piece of the American Dream: A house in the suburbs. Before WWII, that would have remained just a dream, because few Jews owned cars, and many suburbs were closed to Jews. After the War, both barriers fell, and the Jewish migration to suburbia has continued through today.

In the 'burbs, the Jews were spread apart in houses, not clustered together in apartments. They felt the need for community, however, and found it in their synagogue. Membership in the local synagogue became very important to suburban Jewry. However, they didn't join for praying, but for mingling. They didn't attend services, but participated in men's club and sisterhood events.

The synagogue had another function, to train the next generation. The question is: To train them for what? Boys and girls attended synagogue schools for bar- and bat-mitzvah training. The bar-mitzvah was not viewed as a beginning of a boy's Judaism, but rather as a graduation **from** Judaism. Typically, the boy (and sometimes, the girl) had a big party with a lot of gifts. Some of the guys would try to smoke cigarettes, while others would get drunk; old folks would pinch the bar-mitzvah boy's cheeks, while his mother would keep fixing his hair. The highlight was the ceremonial dance with his mother and/or sister.[1]

---

1. I won't make too much fun of the party. I had one like that, and it was a ball. I wore a pimp-like maroon tux, and kept stuffing envelopes with checks in my pocket. Like most bar-mitzvah boys, I was the center of attention, and loved every minute of it.

And then it ended. After age 13, no more Jewish education and no more synagogue services (except for Rosh Hashana and Yom Kippur). The result was the most Jewishly ignorant generation in 3000 years.

So if religion took a back seat to the nouveau suburbanites, what was important to them? A different religion: Materialism. Possessions became very important; not just having them, but acquiring them at a good price. Jews never just show something off; we always have to say how much the object cost.

"Oh, what a beautiful Picasso."

"You like it? Its an original. Picasso wanted $100,000 for it, but I got it for only 75."

In the late '60s, many of the children of suburbia rebelled against the materialism of their parents. They joined groups like the SDS, and planned and plotted campus takeovers and proletarian revolution. Parents wondered where they had gone wrong. Then the '70s arrived. The revolutionaries went to business school, and expressed their rebellion against society through insider trading.

3. The Six-Day War and the Return of Israel

For most of the '50s and '60s, Zionist feelings had been laying dormant in the souls of American Jews. But a seed had been planted some years earlier in the form of the most influential book in American Jewish history: Leon Uris's "Exodus." Thousands of Jews were first turned on to Israel through the reading of that book[1] or the viewing of the movie version.[2] They felt for Israel, but it was far away, not the subject of their immediate concern.

---

1.   Interestingly, years later, Soviet Jews would be turned on to Israel through smuggled copies of "Exodus."
2.   It sure didn't hurt that Paul Newman, blue eyes and all, played Ari Ben-Canaan. More interesting is the fact that the original character of Ari was reportedly based on the late Yitzhak Rabin.

That all changed in May, 1967. For three weeks, Egypt's President Nasser threatened Israel with destruction, and the world didn't care. It forgot the earlier guarantees, the U.N. removed its troops from Sinai, and the Egyptians blockaded the Straits of Tiran. Suddenly, Israel's very survival was a source of immediate concern.

During those three weeks, my seventh grade class went on a tour of the U.N. Someone there thought it would be quite amusing if this group of Jewish day school students were to be led by a Jordanian tour guide. What an ice princess she was. Jeff Cohen, our class "peace-and-love" guy, tried to be friendly. "What's it like in Jordan?" he asked.

She answered coldly, "Why don't you come and see for yourselves?" Little did she know how prophetic those words would be.

American Jewry woke up Monday morning, June 5, 1967 to the news that war had begun. Before we could start worrying (and who worries better than Jews?), the Israeli Air Force had destroyed almost all the enemy planes. In six days, the Sinai, Jerusalem, West Bank, and the Golan Heights were ours.

Pride in Israel knew no bounds, and neither did fundraising. Through the years, the collective American Jewish effort at raising money for Israel during the Six-Day War has achieved mythic proportions. But it's no myth. The war came after the traditional spring fundraising season; yet, American Jews broke their piggy banks (in some cases, literally) to donate to UJA and buy Israel bonds. Never in history had so much money been raised so fast by so few. To use the actual numbers, in 1966, UJA raised $136 million, leading to a Fortune magazine article on "The Miracle of Jewish Giving." Following the Six-Day War, Jews donated $317 million to Israel. That number was eclipsed during the crisis of the Yom Kippur War of 1973, when $675 million was raised.

The UJA raises more money than the **combined** campaigns of the American Heart Association, the American Cancer Society, the Muscular Dystrophy Association, the March of Dimes, and the National Easter Seal Society. Some sectors of the community are better givers than others. Rabbi Irving Koslowe, in his capacity as chaplain of Sing-Sing prison, reported a 100% contribution rate. The local campaign chairman protested, "Honestly, Rabbi, we didn't use any strong-arm tactics."[1]

The war changed American Jewry more than any event since the Great Migration of 1881. From that point on, the American community would become an Israel-centered one. Political behavior, education, culture, fundraising, and literature were all dominated by Israel-based concerns.

That doesn't mean the relationship between the two communities has always been smooth. American Jews were comfortable with Israel's Labor Party, especially when it was led by American Golda Meir (who spoke Hebrew with a strong Midwestern accent). In 1977, however, Menachem Begin and his Likud Party won the national election. Begin, with his Polish accent, formal manner, and right-wing politics, wasn't as easy to warm up to.

In addition, since the Six-Day War, Israel had grown more and more isolated. What American Jews didn't realize was that the years 1945-1967 were an aberration of history. Those years marked the lowest level of world anti-Semitism in history. But the honeymoon was ending. First, Israel betrayed its sympathizers by winning the war in 1967. Next, after the Yom Kippur surprise attack of 1973, Israel committed the sin of successfully counter-attacking and gaining even more Arab territory.

By the time Israel launched the disastrous war in Lebanon in 1982, most of the world was hostile to it. The Christian Arab massacre of Palestinians in the Sabra and Shatila refugee camps led to an orgy of anti-Semitic cartoons and demonstrations, mostly in Europe, but in the U.S. as well. When it came to Israel, American Jews felt they were on the defensive. Israel didn't help matters by its feeble public relations efforts. It seemed that the prerequisite for being on Israel's propaganda team was to have flunked Marketing 101. At the very least, Israel could have pointed out to neutral Americans that the "huge" West Bank was the size of only one or two average American counties (or half the size of one James Baker Texas county).

---

1. This is not surprising. According to Zev Chafets, in his book, "Members of the Tribe," Jewish prisoners, whether incarcerated for fraud, murder, or sexual assault, tend to be very right-wing when it comes to Israel.

Many Jews reacted by increasing their support for Israel through donations to AIPAC, the Israel lobbying group.[1] Others went in the opposite direction, and joined American Friends of Peace Now, where celebrities like Woody ("She's Mia's daughter, not mine") Allen and Richard Dreyfus could harshly criticize Israel from the safety of Manhattan apartments and L.A. houses. After the signing of the Oslo Accords, it was the turn of the right to make fools of themselves, by viciously attacking the Rabin government from Brooklyn. If you don't like the policies of any specific Israeli government, move there and vote the bums out. Netanyahu didn't win with votes from Brooklyn, and Hollywood Jews won't vote him out, so if a government is in power, and you think it stinks, don't run to your local congressman or the New York Times op-ed page to let everyone know your complaints.

In the mid-'80s, Israel embarrassed American Jews in the Jonathan Pollard Affair by recruiting an American Jew to serve as a spy in the United States, raising that old dual loyalty question again. Even worse was Israel's treatment of poor, pathetic Pollard once he was caught. It was like "Mission: Impossible:" "The Secretary will disavow any knowledge of your activities." They disavowed Pollard and left him hanging. Only recently have American Jews realized what a bum rap Pollard got, a life sentence inspired by Casper Weinberger's lies to the judge, despite a favorable plea agreement. Pollard's Israeli handlers, on the other hand, received promotions and cushy jobs.[2]

Yet, as the '90s began, even the most jaded Jew woke up to the importance of Israel. First came the rescue of the ancient Jewish community of Ethiopia in Operation Moses and Operation Solomon. The pictures of Israeli planes saving 20,000 black Jews touched an emotional

---

1. To anti-Semites, AIPAC is today's version of the Elders of Zion.
2. Pollard appealed, naturally, but was screwed when the two Jews on the three-person appellate panel ruled against him, while the sole non-Jew, Judge Stephen Williams, pointed out the unfairness of his sentence. The lead Jewish judge against Pollard: None other than the Honorable Ruth Bader Ginsburg.

chord in the hearts of American Jews. They knew that only one country would rescue the Ethiopian Jews: Israel.

Next came the massive influx of Russian Jews. Through the mid-and late 80s, Russian Jews had been opting to go to the U.S. rather than Israel. This new group of Russian Jewish immigrants was economically, not ideologically, motivated. And Israel was an economic basket case, while America was still the Goldeneh Medina, the Golden Land.

As recession swept over America, however, the government imposed tougher rules regarding the Russian refugees. First, since Israel was open to them, the numbers allowed to come to the U.S. would be limited. Second, the federal government was cutting its aid to refugees; the Jewish communities would now be on their own as far as helping them. All of a sudden, those Jews who always demanded freedom of choice for Soviet Jews realized that their community resources would be greatly strained, if not bankrupted, by the newcomers. Better they should go to Israel.

And that's what happened. Israel accepted the immigrants without a complaint. Of course, in typical Israeli bureaucratic fashion, the government there proceeded to screw things up, but that's another story. The American community once again saw that there was only one haven in this world for Jews: Israel. In the American-Israeli relationship, Israel was again seen as the senior partner.

4. The Emergence of the Holocaust

For years, the Holocaust remained a hidden topic among American Jews, spoken about among survivors, but with no one else. The survivors were too busy making their new lives here and were not yet secure enough in their American-ness to speak openly of their experiences. In Israel, the 1960 Eichmann trial had lifted the veil of silence. However, in the United States, the Holocaust become a hot topic as a result of that most American of institutions: TV.

The mini-series, "Holocaust," introduced millions of Americans to the history of the Final Solution. It also showed the victims not as older,

Yiddish-accented Jews, but as attractive American-types like James Woods and Tovah Feldshuh. Also, by this time, the survivors had lost their insecurity. They began speaking out, writing memoirs, and erecting monuments. College courses on the Holocaust became popular in Judaic studies department throughout the nation. A survivor, Tom Lantos, was elected to Congress, as was a member of "the second generation," Sam Gejdenson.

A number of books appeared, documenting the psychological problems of Holocaust survivors and their children. The implication of these studies was that survivors and their children were full of neuroses as a result of their and their parents' experiences. But was that really so?

Speaking as a member of the second generation, my answer is, Usually, no (at least I don't think **I'm** neurotic, but who knows?). The Holocaust's affect on a survivor depends on that person's experiences. A person who was older, who lost his wife and children, and who spent the War years in a concentration camp, will be more greatly affected by the Holocaust than someone who was young, single, and in the partisans. Similarly, the less affected the parent, the less affected the child.

And don't forget the Lottie Gleicher Rule, named for my mother who first told it to me: Someone who had mental problems before the War wasn't going to become normal through his Holocaust experiences. Finally, because the younger the survivor, the better off he is psychologically, the majority of today's survivors are quite normal. Remember, it's been 50 years since the Holocaust, and many of the older survivors (about one-third of the original 140,000 refugees as of 1997) have died of old age.

The survivors became part of the American Jewish community and achieved material success even faster than earlier immigrant groups. The only major difference I have noted between survivors and other American Jews relates to Israel: Survivors are fanatically pro-Israel, and will tolerate no criticism of it (unless that criticism remains "in the family."). You won't find many survivors among American Friends of Peace Now. (Yes, I know I'm picking on them again, but they're so pick-on-able.)

We are starting to see some criticism of all the attention and emphasis being placed on the Holocaust. Should the Holocaust be the defining Jewish experience for young American Jews? Should every dinky city in America spend money on its own individual Holocaust museum and memorial while Yad Vashem (Israel's national Holocaust memorial) goes begging for funds and Jewish education in America remains woefully underfunded? The debate continues (but note the prejudicial way I asked the questions).

5. Jews and Politics

Considering that Jews make up less than 2½% of the U.S. population, politicians pay a lot of attention to what we think. Why is that? As they say in the real estate world: Location, location, location. Jews are concentrated in those key states with a lot of electoral votes. In 1988, Bush won California with less than 51% of the vote. In a close race, the votes of the 600,000 California Jews could prove decisive.

For the most part, Jews vote Democratic. That wasn't always the case. The German Jews, inspired by the memory of Abe Lincoln, were staunch Republicans. The East European Jews, however, lived in the domain of big city Democratic machines like Tammany Hall, and voted accordingly.

Jews had participated in politics even before the age of mass immigration. Twenty Jews were elected to Congress between 1820-1880. Bernard Goldsmith and Philip Wasserman served as mayors of Portland, Oregon. Morris Goodman was a member of Los Angeles's first city council.

Contrary to popular belief, it took the Russian immigrants quite a while to get the hang of the political process. As late as 1912, the mostly-Jewish 8th Assembly District in lower Manhattan had the city's lowest percentage of registered voters. But once the Jews caught the political bug, they became active participants in the process.

In 1916, the Republican influence among Jews was still strong enough to give Charles Evans Hughes 45% of their vote against the Jewish hero, Woodrow Wilson (that is, hero to the Jews; despite the fact that he was an intellectual, Wilson, of course, wasn't Jewish). Even Warren Harding got 43% of the Jewish vote in 1920. But times were changing. In 1928, New York Governor Al Smith received 72% of the Jewish vote. Smith, an Irishman, was raised on the Lower East Side, and had such a heavy New York accent as to sound like a TV sit-com character. Unlike other New York Irish political leaders, he cared about more than merely local issues, and tried to involve the Jews in the political process. The Jews loved him.

The final conversion of the Jews came in 1932, with the election of another Jewish hero, FDR. Roosevelt received 90% of the Jewish vote in his last two elections, as the Jews became permanent Democrats.

After WWII, Jews made money and moved to the suburbs, but still remained Democrats. The saying about Jews was that they had the incomes of Episcopalians, and the voting records of Puerto Ricans. To many Jews, being a liberal Democrat and being a good Jew were synonymous. In fact, growing up in the Bronx, I never met a Jewish Republican until I got to college.

In the '70s, however, it was the issue of Israel that caused a shift among Jewish attitudes. When George McGovern was nominated for president in 1972, many Jews were uncomfortable with his perceived weakness on Israel. Nixon, long regarded as poison to the Jews, received 35% of their vote. That was the highest Republican percentage in 52 years, except for war-hero Eisenhower.

Carter got the Jewish vote back in 1976, but lost it in 1980, as Reagan received 39% (but down to 31% in 1984). Finally, in 1988, Bush won 27% of the Jewish vote, showing James Baker's ignorance when he said "F___ 'em. They didn't vote for us anyway." Sorry, Baker, we did – and were we dumb! Jews made up for it in 1992 and 1996, when they voted overwhelmingly for pro-Israel Bill Clinton. George Bush received the lowest percentage of the Jewish vote a national candidate has gotten since these statistics were counted.

The rise of the Jewish vote for Republicans was a direct result of concern over Israel. Until 1992, the Democrats were seen as soft on defense, and willing to tolerate anti-Israel forces like that of Jesse Jackson (more on him later). The Israel issue became the litmus test for politicians seeking the Jewish vote no matter what office involved.

An example of this is the 1982 Illinois gubernatorial race between incumbent Republican Jim Thompson and Democrat Adlai Stevenson. Stevenson's record in the U.S. Senate showed a marked coldness to Israel.[1] Thompson, on the other hand, had many Jewish friends, was a regular on the Israel fundraising dinner circuit, and impressed many as a sincere friend of Israel and Jewish causes. Thompson defeated Stevenson by only 5,000 votes. An examination of the voting patterns in the usually Democratic Jewish areas in Chicago's north side and north suburbs shows a drop off in the vote for Stevenson. This drop was enough to get Thompson re-elected.

This election showed a key to keeping the Jewish vote important: Reward friends, punish enemies, and re-read Machiavelli's "The Prince" once a year. If a candidate spends three years attacking Israel, and wakes up during election season, giving him our votes is counterproductive. (Sorry, Bob Dole.) Groups like AIPAC, the Israel lobby, now keep tabs on Congressmen all year, making it easier to tell who's a friend and who's a foe.

As I said earlier, location of the Jewish voters is an essential reason why we're so heavily courted in presidential races. Another reason applies to all elections: PAC money. Jews, recognizing the importance of Congress to Israel, are willing to put their money where their mouths are and give generously to political action committees dedicated to supporting candidates friendly to Israel. Since money is the mother's milk of politics, few candidates are willing to cut off the cash cow.

Many Jews are uneasy with this emphasis on Israel above all other issues, and would like Jewish voters to examine candidates on a range of issues. Just because a certain senator always votes with Israel, should we support him if we disagree with him on every other issue? All things being

---

1. No surprise there. During the 1930s, Stevenson's father, the future 1952/1956 presidential candidate and darling of Jewish liberal voters, complained to a friend that Jews in Washington were too prominent and autocratic.

equal, we will vote for a candidate whose positions on **all** issues matches our own. However, if one candidate is strong on Israel and the other is soft, Jews will usually support the pro-Israel candidate even if the other one is more in tune with us on other issues.

6. Jewish-Americans and African-Americans

Jews and Blacks: What went wrong? Weren't Jews the founders of the NAACP? Didn't Jews give their lives in the South for Black civil rights? Didn't we both believe in freedom and equality? So why do we hate each others' guts today?

Some Jews believe the myth that all Blacks loved us until the late '60s. That's just not so. In 1943, a race riot broke out in Harlem. Even back then, one of the central features of the violence was the anti-Semitic feelings expressed by the mob, a precursor to the riots of the next generation.

The early '60s was the high point of Black-Jewish cooperation. One-half of the civil rights attorneys in the South were Jews, as were 1/2 of the Freedom Riders, and 2/3 of the white volunteers during Freedom Summer. Rabbis like Abraham Joshua Heschel marched arm-in-arm with Martin Luther King. King himself was one of the reasons for this interracial friendliness. Unlike later Black leaders, King always voiced support for Israel and Jews. But even before King's death in 1968, the alliance was breaking up.

First, the Jewish perspective: Inner-city Jews never saw a Black-Jewish alliance. That was for liberal Jews in the suburbs who sent their kids to all-white schools and never saw a Black face in the streets. The Jews of the cities saw Blacks in a different light. To them, Blacks meant crime and ruined neighborhoods. A Jew who ran away from East Flatbush (Brooklyn) or Laurelton (Queens) or South Shore (Chicago) or Mattapan (Boston) saw Blacks as objects of fear and hate, not compassion and sympathy.[1]

---

1.   As a result, Jews run away from a neighborhood whenever they see a Black person

Next, the Black perspective: Younger Blacks felt patronized by the Jewish attitude that they, the Jews, were the inspiration for and the leaders of the civil rights movement. They saw Jews doing things **for** Blacks, not **with** Blacks. The younger activists' desire to take charge of their own destiny resulted in a disparagement of any Jewish effort to help.

The end of the alliance came in 1968. Brooklyn's Ocean Hill-Brownsville local school board sought to fire most of its Jewish teachers. As a result, the teachers' union went out on strike. New York became a seething cauldron of Black-Jewish hate, led, in Jewish eyes, by Black radio host Julius Lester, who allowed his show to be used as a forum for anti-Semitism.[1]

For the next decade, the two groups had an uneasy cold peace, marked by divisions over affirmative action, Israel's relations with South Africa, and Israel in general. However, the '80s saw the cold peace return to hostility.

The chief culprit was Jesse Jackson, who had become the number one Black leader in 1984 with his run for president. Unlike King, Jackson did not like Jews and did not like Israel. Yet Blacks were insulted when virtually all Jews worked against Jackson. This wasn't the '60s anymore, when a guilt-ridden liberal Jewish population would excuse Jesse's antics. It was the '80s; if you were against **us**, we were against **you**.

Jackson was just the tip of the iceberg. His ally, Louis Farrakhan, who flaunted his anti-Semitic beliefs, packed auditoriums throughout America, attracting enthusiastic crowds. In New York, City College

---

move in. However, if Jews move to a neighborhood where Blacks are already living, that's okay, because "they must have spent a lot of money for their house." Therefore, my modest proposal to achieve stable Jewish neighborhoods is as follows: No Jew should be allowed to move into a new neighborhood unless preceded by at least two Black families. The Jews will see Blacks already there, and will say, "Oh yeah, Blacks live here, no big deal."

1. Lester was so taken aback by the attacks on him that he started studying Judaism to see what all the fuss was about. He later converted to Judaism, and was forced out of the Afro-American Studies Department at UMass, because a Jew, even a Black Jew, didn't belong there.

Professor Lionel Jeffries blamed Jews for a variety of Black grievances. Finally, these feelings boiled over in Brooklyn's Crown Heights neighborhood in a full-fledged anti-Jewish pogrom in 1992.

Surveys have shown that Blacks are the only ethnic group in America in which anti-Semitism **increases** with educational level. Is there any hope of a reconciliation between the two groups?

Possibly. Right now, things look pessimistic, but historically, Jews had horrible relations with other ethnic groups (mostly Catholic), relations which are now smooth. Eventually, a new generation of Black leaders will emerge, those secure enough not to blame Jews for every evil under the sun. On the other hand, Jews cannot tell African-Americans who their leaders should be. If Blacks want Farrakhan, that is their choice, not ours. Every time a Jewish group denounces Farrakhan, he gains an edge over other African-American leaders. In dealing with the Black community, Jews must extend the hand of friendship only to those who are willing to take it in the same spirit. We must deal with African-Americans like we deal with any other hyphenated American: If you want our friendship, you must act like a friend, despite the differences between us.

7. Jews and American Civilization

This is the part where we get to brag. By "American Civilization," I mean all aspects of life that make up America: Culture, the professions, sports, etc. Without Jews, life in America would be deficient in so many ways it boggles the mind.

Take the most American of all modern culture: The movies. They were invented by Thomas Edison, but refined by Jews: Adolph Zukor, Samuel Goldwyn, Harry Cohn, Louis B. Mayer, the Warner Brothers, and others. These men created "America" in the eyes of the nation. Coming here as poor immigrants, they imagined that the "real" America was a land of small towns, with happy families, living in white houses, surrounded by picket fences. In short, Andy Hardy-ville. Because that was the America presented in the movies, that was the America most Americans thought was real.

Jews never appeared in these movies. The immigrant studio heads were too insecure about themselves to mention the word "Jew" in a movie. Many of them wanted to forget their Judaism. They divorced their wives and married budding starlets (of the non-Jewish variety). Interestingly, when Zukor, the last of the pioneers, died at the age of 102, a search of his office found his tallit and tefilin tucked in the closet. He had kept them with him since his arrival in America over 80 years earlier.

Today's movie business is still dominated by Jews: Michael Eisner revived a dying Disney. Steven Spielberg created a new movie empire. Super-agent Michael Ovitz became the single most powerful man in Hollywood. Unlike their predecessors, today's movie Jews aren't ashamed of their religion. They donate big to UJA and other causes. Even before making "Schindler's List," Spielberg had an entire movie archives named for him at Hebrew University.

Jews also dominate other entertainment fields: Television's three networks were founded by William Paley (CBS), David Sarnoff (NBC), and Leonard Goldenson (ABC). Look at the credits of any TV show: Either the writer, producer, or director (or some combination of them) will be Jewish.

As for live entertainment, Jews haven't been big as rock performers, with the notable exception of Bob Dylan. Classical music is another story. America's greatest conductor was Leonard Bernstein, and greatest composer was George Gershwin (if you don't think Rhapsody in Blue is the greatest classical piece by an American, you're either a barbarian or a snob).

Another form of entertainment is comedy. From Jack Benny and George Burns to Woody Allen and Lenny Bruce to Jerry Seinfeld and Gary Shandling, comedy in America has been a Jewish profession.[1] It is to their

---

1. I don't mean to overlook the most underrated Jewish humorists of all, The Three Stooges.

credit that Bob Hope, Eddie Murphy, Jay Leno and others have managed to overcome the burden of not being Jewish to succeed at this art form.

Jews are good at teaching other Americans about culture and entertainment. Jews have taught people how to dance (Arthur Murray), how to evaluate movies (Gene Siskel,[1] Michael Medved, and many others), how to read a book (Mortimer Adler), how to understand classical music (Leonard Bernstein and Aaron Copland), how to play chess (Fred Reinfeld), and, in general, how to behave (Dear Abby, Ann Landers, and Ms. Manners).

Jews have been less dominant in the field of sports. Sure, individual Jews were stars in baseball (Hank Greenberg and Sandy Koufax), football (Sid Luckman and Marshall Goldberg), and boxing (Barney Ross and Benny Leonard), but in only one sport was the Jewish contribution critical: Basketball.

Basketball is **the** city game, and Jews, being **the** city people, gravitated towards it from its inception. It was a mostly Jewish group that formed the NBA in 1946, led by its first commissioner, Maurice Podoloff. Only one Jew, Dolph Schayes, has ever been a dominant NBA star, but the team owners have remained mostly Jewish. In 1980, when the entire league was on the verge of collapse, it was David Stern, the new commissioner, who built it into a new powerhouse, with Magic Johnson, Larry Bird, and Michael Jordan as the foundation.

Now we turn to the "Jewish" fields: Law and medicine. Today, Jews are almost as dominant in the legal field as in entertainment. Some, like Judge Wapner, fall within both areas. Pull out the faculty list of any major law school in the U.S., and you will see the large numbers of Jewish professors. Look at any list of the greatest justices of the U.S. Supreme Court, and you will see the names of Brandeis, Cardozo, and Frankfurter. The most influential judges and legal thinkers are usually Jews. Finally, one of the most famous private attorneys in America today is Mr. Chutzpah himself, Alan Dershowitz.

---

1. The skinny one; Ebert is the fat one.

Medicine has been a Jewish profession since before the Middle Ages. In medieval Spain, despite Church rules forbidding Catholics to use Jewish physicians, nobles considered it a sign of class to have a Jewish doctor. That attitude is true in today's United States, as reflected by the Archie Bunker idea: Even if you don't like Jews, you want a Jewish doctor.

Contemporary medical training is entirely the idea of Abraham Flexner, a Jewish doctor who reformed primitive medical education into the form it is today.[1] Doctors usually don't achieve the fame of lawyers, but it could be argued that the most famous doctor of the 20th century was Jonas Salk, discover of the polio vaccine. Another indication of Jewish importance in this field is a review of the list of American Nobel Medicine Prize winners; a huge proportion are Jewish.[2]

Saving the worst for last, we have Jewish contributions to modern crime. As I have stated earlier, Jews don't usually shoot, mug, assault or rape other people. Jews have always been more adept at white collar crime, that is, stealing without physically injuring anyone. This past decade saw the Jewish criminal as the insider trader: Ivan Boesky, Dennis Levine, Michael Milken. Their actions, in causing the destruction of many corporations, hurt many innocent people, and violated not only U.S. securities laws, but the laws of Jewish ethics as well (see Leviticus [Vayikra] 19:14, and its commentaries). Unfortunately, they pursued the American dream more like mob guys Arnold Rothstein and Meyer Lansky, rather than like noted Jewish businessmen like Julius (Sears Roebuck) Rosenwald, Laurence (CBS) Tisch, and others.

When it comes to legitimate business, Jews have been very successful. The Forbes 400 list of the 400 richest Americans should, statistically, have only 10 Jews on it. Instead, there are 100, ten times the Jewish population percentage.

As this brief review has shown, without the Jewish contribution, the United States would be a much more boring country. An interesting

---

1. Interns on 36-hour shifts would claim that medical education is still primitive.
2. Overall, 27% of all U.S. Nobel laureates are Jews, ten times the general Jewish population percentage.

question is whether there is some genetic factor in the Jewish people that leads to such contributions, or is it all a product of environment? One thing is for sure: It is a lack of Jewish ethics that leads to behavior like insider trading. Therefore, the better Jew a person is, the more likely that his or her contribution to American society will be a positive one.[1]

8. American Jews and Their Religion(s)

American Jews are divided into five distinct religious branches: Reform (about 25%), Conservative (about 30%), Reconstructionist (about 5%), Orthodox (about 10%), and Apathetic (about 30%). While the Apathetic branch is the fastest growing, I'll limit this discussion to the first four groups. Don't worry; there's enough criticism for each one.

A. Reform

Reform today is very different than it was years ago, when it was in its "classical" mode. Back then, anything that smacked of being "too Jewish" was forbidden. To illustrate this point, we should go back to Yom Kippur of 1960, when I was six. I attended services at a small Orthodox shul in the Bronx (vernacular translation: I "davened" in a "shteibel"). During a break, my father asked whether I'd like to see what services looked like at Tremont Temple a few blocks away. We entered the Temple lobby and looked inside, organ music reverberating in the background.

An usher approached. "Gentlemen, if you want to go in, you'll have to take off your hats."

I asked, "What hats?"

---

1. An interesting question is this: With all the great achievements of Jews in America, why is Israeli public life so screwed up? The answer is obvious. In America, we over-achieved to "impress the goyim." In Israel, there are no non-Jews to impress. Sure, there are Arabs, but they're not real goyim – WASPS. The answer to Israel's problems is to encourage aliya to Israel of American non-Jews. Then, there would be a Gentile community to impress, and Jews would work much harder.

He said, "The ones you're wearing."

What we were wearing were yarmulkes. I looked at my father, and said, "Dad, let's get out of here."

Tremont Temple no longer exists (it's probably Tremont African Methodist Evangelical Temple now), and neither does Reform's disdain for Judaism. In fact, Reform has been returning to Tradition for quite some time now, a very positive development. In Israel, Reform is even more traditional than in the States.

But what is the future of Reform? Most Reform young people are intermarrying out of the faith, leaving a smaller Reform Jewish group. Reform is trying to counter this by accepting as Jews those born of a Jewish father. All that this stop-gap measure does is drive a wedge between Reform and the other branches of Judaism, which recognize only the children of Jewish mothers as Jews.

Reform's problem is that it has not defined what it is that makes up a religious Reform Jew. Naturally, it is something different than a religious Orthodox or Conservative Jew, but what is it? Does one exist? Reform must find out what it wants from its adherents, both as to belief and practice. Then it must make provisions for teaching its children based on those values. Sunday and congregational schools are proven failures, so Reform must set up its own day school system if it wants to exist by the year 2054. Reform day schools are just now sprouting in various parts of the country, but dozens more are needed.

Despite my traditional beliefs (or maybe because of them), I'm rooting for Reform to get its act together. A Reform branch with no doctrine and no day schools will not survive, and that would be a loss to the Jewish people as a whole.

B. Conservative

Since the end of WWII, Conservatism has been the branch with the largest number of American Jews. It grew because it was seen as the middle-of-the-road belief: Not cold classical Reform, not Yiddish, ritualistic Orthodoxy. Another coup was a decision of the Jewish Theological

Seminary's Law Committee to allow driving on the Sabbath, but only to and from the synagogue. That allowed Conservatism to be the perfect religion for spread-out suburbia.[1]

Today, however, Conservatism is afflicted by problems. Like Reform, it is losing its young people. Like Reform, it is confused as to how it should be defined, that is, what exactly is a religious Conservative Jew? Dennis Prager, one of the brightest American Jewish thinkers today (despite being from Southern California), has pointed out that Orthodoxy will always be seen as the only **true** branch of Judaism, as long as there are no religious Reform and Conservative Jews.

Conservatism has the biggest gap between the clergy and the laity. In Reform, the rabbi and the congregation usually have the same level of observance and/or belief. The same is true in Orthodoxy. However, in Conservatism, the rabbi is usually an observant religious Jew, leading a congregation where no one else is, a disheartening experience. Part of the problem is that too many synagogues are theaters, where the rabbi and cantor put on a show for a passive audience of congregants. Some synagogues, influenced by either the Havurah movement of the '60s or led by dynamic rabbis, are changing this, but a revolution is needed.

Conservatism has a brighter future than Reform because many of the important building blocks are already in place. Camp Ramah has been a key in strengthening Jewish belief among Conservative youth. The Solomon Schechter Day Schools are growing by leaps and bounds, but there should be many more of them. Most Conservative rabbis, unwilling to upset their complacent congregants, fail to push them to send their kids to Schechter. However, a day school education is the future, not the synagogue school.

Conservatism has always believed in the primacy of Jewish law (Halacha), with the ability to change. That change has led to tensions in the movement, especially over the question of the ordination of women.

---

1. Conservative congregants interpreted this decision as allowing driving to the mall on the way home from Sabbath services. Eventually, the synagogue portion of the Saturday drive was dropped, but the mall portion was retained.

Many on the right-wing of Conservatism split off to form the Union of Traditional Judaism. Without this anchor, will Conservatism drift in the direction of Reform? Will Ramah and Schechter be enough to keep the movement growing into the 21st century? Will there be a growth of committed Conservative Jews, so that Conservative rabbis of the future won't be the only religious Jews in their congregations? Beats me. To paraphrase a Jewish proverb, since the destruction of the Temple, prophecy has been granted only to fools.

C. Reconstructionism

Reconstructionism is the least-understood of America's Jewish branches. It was developed by Mordecai Kaplan, one of the most important religious leaders in American Jewish history. Kaplan was an Orthodox rabbi (ordained in the last pre-Schechter class at the Seminary), who was one of the founders of the Young Israel movement. He taught at JTS for 50 years and influenced hundreds of rabbinical students there. He was viewed by Orthodoxy as a heretic, who formed his own religion.

That religion was Reconstructionism. Kaplan believed that Judaism was more than its laws (that is, the Halacha), it was a civilization. Judaism encompassed all aspects of the Jewish experience: Laws, history, culture, language. Kaplan's philosophy was expressed in the Jewish Center type of synagogue. Such a synagogue wasn't just for prayers, but was for meetings, classes, activities, and sports. Today, the best example of a Kaplan-type environment would be the Jewish Community Center (JCC), with its wide range of Jewish activities.

Because Judaism was more than Halacha, Kaplan felt free to experiment. He instituted the concept of a bat-mitzvah for 12-year-old girls in 1922 for his daughter Judith (who celebrated the 70th anniversary of that occasion in 1992). He allowed women to be called to the Torah, and to be ordained. As for God, He/She was not seen by Kaplan as the personal and supernatural God of Tradition, but as a force in the world. In fact, Obiwan Kenobee of Star Wars is a true Reconstructionist when he states as his credo, "May the Force be with you."

Reconstructionism has influenced **all** of the other branches of Judaism, especially in its treatment of women and its expansion of the role of the synagogue. Kaplan, however, wanted to remain within Conservatism, and refused for years to form his own branch. Finally, he gave in, and established the Reconstructionist Rabbinical Seminary in Philadelphia. This was soon followed by a congregational organization for Reconstructionist Synagogues.

Despite his revolutionary activities, Kaplan himself prayed in the traditional manner (in a tallit and tefilin) every day. He died at the age of 102, active to the end.

As for Reconstructionism, it has an uncertain future despite its growth. Many of its ideas have been taken over by Reform and Conservatism. So its first order of business is to define what makes it different. Its next problem is the next generation. It has no day schools, so where will the new Reconstructionists come from? Most likely, from other branches of Judaism, but is that enough of a base for the future? If Conservatism, without its right-wing group, veers leftward, it is possible that the Reconstructionist movement will come back home, giving it a more solid base.

D. *Orthodoxy*

A personal aside: I was born and raised Orthodox, am a member of an Orthodox synagogue (though my kids went to a Conservative day school), and thus know this branch the best. It also means that this is the branch of which I am most critical.

Before WWII, despite the existence of Yeshiva College, Orthodoxy was on the ropes. Its followers were dying out, and, for young people, Conservatism was the wave of the future. Most newly-ordained rabbis were accepting pulpits in synagogues where men and women sat together, the Reform/Conservative custom.

This all changed after the War. The Holocaust refugees revitalized Orthodoxy in the United States. Today, despite making up only 10% of the American Jewish population, Orthodoxy is in no danger of dying out. In fact, it is growing more than ever. There are day schools and yeshivas throughout the country. Scholarly books are available in English translation, making Torah study accessible to more Jews than ever. So what's the problem?

The problem is that it isn't Orthodoxy that is growing, but strictness; not Torah-Judaism, but right-wing rigidity. Part of this is a result of post-Holocaust demographics. Before the War, the center of Judaism was in Poland, from Lithuania in the north to Galicia in the south. Hungarian Judaism was in the minor leagues, influenced by Rabbi Moses Schreiber, known as the Chasam Sofer.[1] The Chasam Sofer stated, "anything new is forbidden by the Torah" (which is quite a witty pun in the original Hebrew), and Hungarian Judaism was known for its stringency.

During the Holocaust, over 90% of Polish Jewry was murdered. Fortunately, Hitler didn't turn to Hungarian Jews until 1944. Even with the Germans' most determined efforts, half the Hungarian Jewish community survived. The result was that harsh Hungarian Orthodoxy assumed more importance and influence than it ever had before. It's like the St. Louis Browns, baseball's worst franchise. In 1944, the Browns finally won the pennant because the other teams had been decimated by the War. Hungarian Orthodoxy is Judaism's version of the 1944 St. Louis Browns, a poor representative of the real thing, on top due to circumstances beyond anyone's control.

In Orthodoxy, everyone is always looking over their shoulders to make sure they're observant enough. The yeshivas that were established in America after the War got more and more rigid; after all, they didn't want to be accused of being too modern. As for modern Orthodoxy, represented by Yeshiva University, it was on the defensive. In fact, today, modern Orthodoxy refuses to use that term. It now calls itself "Centrist Orthodoxy." The term "modern" is, well, too modern.

---

1. Jewish scholars are always called by the names of their most famous books. In this case, everyone refers to "the Chasam Sofer," a book title, rather than to Rabbi Schreiber, his real name. It is as if Americans referred to James Michener as "the South Pacific" or Stephen King as "the Shining."

There are some basic differences between Centrist/Modern Orthodoxy and the Right:

1) Israel – Centrists believe in Israel as the center of the Jewish world. Its establishment is seen as an act of God, and Israel Independence Day is celebrated as a religious holiday. The right sees Israel as a center of Jews and Torah learning, but places no special religious connotation on the **State** of Israel or Independence Day.

2) Secular studies – Centrists believe that secular studies have value in and of themselves; the Right believes that secular studies merely serve the purpose of enabling a person to earn a living.

3) Women: Centrists accept ceremonies like bat-mitzvahs, and some even accept women's prayer groups. The Right believes that such ceremonies are unacceptable innovations. Unfortunately, in this area, as in many others, the rise of Conservatism has taken the pressure off Orthodoxy to be innovative. Those people who would press for changes within the Halacha get disgusted and turn to Conservatism. The Right is more than happy to be rid of these "troublemakers."

4) Relations with other Jews: Centrists want to reach out to non-Orthodox Jews as equals. The Right sees them as virtual non-believers, or, at best, candidates for proselytizing.

5) Rabbis: Centrists respect and revere their rabbinical leaders, especially the late Rabbi Joseph Soloveitchik. However, rabbis, though respected for their learning and personal qualities, are not perfect, especially in areas out of their expertise. The Right has adopted a doctrine of rabbinical infallibility (called "Daas Torah"), which, like papal infallibility, is a modern (yes, modern) innovation. Whatever a rabbi says about **any** issue is 100% correct. So we had situations where a noted rabbinical leader refused to issue a ban on cigarette smoking because rabbis before him thought the habit wasn't unhealthy, totally ignoring 30 years of medical research.

Will this growth of the Right at the expense of the Left continue? In fact, will there be any Modern Orthodoxy at all in a few decades? Right now, speaking as a Modern Orthodox Jew, a minority of a minority, it is easy to be pessimistic. However, history teaches us that events and trends are cyclical. In 20 years, Modern Orthodoxy may again be ascendant. Until then, I'll keep a light on for it.[1]

9. Intermarriage: How Many American Jews Will There Be in 2054?

Intermarriage is today's hottest topic among concerned American Jews. Of course, **un**concerned American Jews are the ones intermarrying. Interfaith marriage has been a source of worry since the Jewish community began. Remember David Einhorn? He was the Radical Reformer who criticized Isaac Mayer Wise for being too timid about reforms. Here's what Einhorn said about intermarriage in 1870: To lend a hand to intermarriage was "to furnish a nail to the coffin of the small Jewish race." Einhorn certainly doesn't sound like the type of Reform rabbi who would officiate at a marriage ceremony with a Protestant minister.

Some statistics: From 1776-1840, the intermarriage rate was 28.7%. Why? Not enough Jews, especially Jewish women. So guys married non-Jews, and that's why there are so few descendants of the original Sephardim.

In 1912, at the height of the East European immigration, there were plenty of Jews around. The intermarriage rate reflected that: 2% (and that was factoring in the German Jews). That rate slowly but surely started growing, picking up speed in the 70s and 80s. Today, the intermarriage rate is a whopping 52%.

---

1. When asked to describe my own affiliation, I cite author Ari Goldman, who referred to himself as a 1950s modern Orthodox Jew.

It is that last number that has caused the uproar. Things are worse than that, however. The rate among younger Jews is much more than 52%. Why is the rate so high, and what can the community do about it?

First, the rate is so high because this is America. Young Jews go to high school and college with young people of all ethnicities and religions, and discover that these non-Jews aren't Cossacks, but people with many ideals and aspirations similar to ours. There is a lot more emotion in love than religion. It is a rare case where someone will say, "I love Mary Pat/Anthony, but I must do my religious duty and break up with her/him." At best, he or she will say, "I love Mary Pat/Anthony) and will try to help her/him see the beauty of Judaism and convert."

The second reason relates to those two principal sources of American culture and information: TV and movies. While there are more Jewish characters on TV and in the movies than ever before, none of these Jews are allowed to fall in love with or marry another Jew (one exception: "Crossing Delancey"). Look at "Thirtysomething": Not only was Michael married to Hopeshiksa, but his cousin, Melissa, dated only non-Jews during the show's run. TV and movies influence America, and the message they put forth is that relationships between Jewish men and women don't exist.[1]

The only way to combat intermarriage is to raise the kind of young people who will be so Jewish in their lives (though not necessarily observant) as to make an intimate relationship with a non-Jew virtually impossible, unless, of course, the non-Jew becomes a Jew. There are two basic ways to achieve that: 1) Jewish education and 2) Israel.

1) There are no statistics on this, but common sense will have to suffice. Someone who gets an elementary day school education will have a much lower probability of intermarriage than someone whose Jewish education was in a synagogue supplemental school (that is, a bar-mitzvah factory).

---

1. These ideas were discussed in detail by Michael Medved in a speech to a meeting of Jewish librarians in July, 1992. Medved's talk was excellent, and some of his thoughts are found in his new book, "Hollywood versus America," and in his article on the same topic in the August, 1996 issue of Moment magazine.

Someone who goes to a Jewish high school lowers the probability even more. Jewish education gives a young person the philosophical background to understand why he/she is a Jew, and why it is important. Of course, Jewish education is not a guarantee, and even Yeshiva University graduates have been known to intermarry, but at least you're increasing the odds towards the Jewish side. The ideal solution would be free day school education, but let's not get too Utopian.

2) Even if the day school option is rejected (it **is** an expensive option), another method of instilling Jewish pride is a year in Israel. The form that that year should take varies: Kibbutz, Hebrew University, yeshiva, etc. The important thing is that a full year in an environment where Judaism is a natural state of affairs can help a young person sort out his/her own feelings about his/her Jewish identity. What does being Jewish mean? Why be Jewish? A year in Israel may not give the answers, but at least it may start the questions.

One possible solution is not really a viable one today: The home. That used to be the answer. A strong Jewish home equaled a strong Jew. But we must be realistic. There are too many other influences around today. The home atmosphere helps, but only in conjunction with the other factors.

As I said before, America is an open society. Even committed Jews will meet and fall in love with non-Jews. However, if these non-Jews convert, an intermarriage loss becomes a conversion gain. Unfortunately, the entire conversion question has been turned into an Israeli political issue, with non-Orthodox converts being viewed as not kosher enough. There should be three basic standards imposed on potential converts: 1) He/she must sincerely want to become a part of Judaism and the Jewish people; 2) He/she must have scored in the 90th percentile on the SATs; and 3) He/she must be reasonably attractive. At least **my** standards address the truly important factors.

So will there be American Jews around to celebrate the community's 400th anniversary in 2054? Yes, but it will be a much smaller community, both in actual numbers and, especially, in percentage. The raw population numbers are scary. The 1991 National Jewish Population Survey found 4.4 million Jews by birth and religion and another 1.1 million Jews who said they had no religion, for a total of 5.5 million "core" Jews. Even within this core group, only 1/2 belong to a synagogue and less than 1/5 give to Jewish causes.

Our numbers are declining. From 1970-1984, the Jewish population in the U.S. declined by about 250,000. Our percentage of the general American population is getting even smaller: From 3.7% in 1937 to 3% in 1961 to less than 2½% in 1997. By 2054, Jews will probably make up less than 1% of the U.S. population. Who will care about the Jewish vote then? Israel had better be self-sufficient or it'll be in big trouble.

Bibliography

This book is a survey, not a detailed text. Therefore, it is my responsibility to direct you to further readings in American Jewish history, from where I derived all my facts, figures, and biased opinions.

- Barry Holtz has edited an excellent bibliography called, "The Schocken Guide to Jewish Books." It includes a section on American Jewish history edited by Jonathan Sarna that is more extensive than this chapter.

- There are four single-volume histories of American Jews that stand out. The most straightforward is "Zion in America," by Henry Feingold, noted professor at City University. "Haven and Hope," by my fellow Yeshiva U. alumnus Abraham Karp, includes documents and readings from the various periods.

- "The Jews in America," by Arthur Hertzberg, was quite controversial when it appeared a few years ago due to Hertzberg's pessimistic and grouchy opinions regarding American Jewry. To my horror, I found myself in agreement with much of his views. The most recent work, "A History of the Jews of America," by Howard Sachar, is the largest of the four, over 1,000 pages. It is very comprehensive as to the past fifty years, and is heavy enough to be used to build up your biceps.

• More ambitious in scope than the other histories is the five-volume "History of the Jews of America," edited by Henry Feingold (again), and published under the auspices of the American Jewish Historical Society. The volumes in that series are the following: "A Time for Planting," by Eli Faber; "A Time for Gathering," by Hasia Dinur; "A Time for Building," by Gerald Sorin; "A Time for Searching," by Henry Feingold (yet again); and "A Time for Healing," by Edward Shapiro. Shapiro is the best and most opinionated writer of the five. That's okay, since I agree with most of his opinions.

• Other general histories include "The American Jewish Experience," edited by Jonathan Sarna, a series of topical readings on American Jewish history. The diminutive Sarna (the Muggsy Bogues of Jewish historians) is one of the leading younger scholars in this field, along with Jeff Gurock, Benny Kraut, Marc Raphael, and others, who I hope will not be upset if I've inadvertently left them out.

• For pictures of many of the people and events discussed in this book, see "An American Jewish Album," by Allon Schoener. The best collection of documents in this field is "A Documentary History of the Jews of the United States 1654-1875," edited by Morris Schappes.

• In a category all by himself is Jacob Rader Marcus, the dean of American Jewish historians. Born in 1896, Marcus has published works on all aspects of the field. In 1991, the first two books of his four-volume set, "United States Jewry, 1776-1985" were published. I was quite impressed that a 95-year-old could still produce a major contribution to the study of history – until I found out that Marcus had completed "United States Jewry" years earlier, when he was only a youthful 92. Marcus was, like his late colleague, Salo Baron, that rare example of a scholar who remains sharp and productive into his 90s. He distilled "United States Jewry" into a one-volume abridgment, "The American Jew". He also complemented the Schappes reader with "The Jew in the American World: A Source Book." Marcus died on November 14, 1995 at the age of 99.

- Isaac Leeser finally has a proper biography, by Lance Sussman entitled "Isaac Leeser and the Making of American Judaism." "The Jews of Chicago," by Irving Cutler, tells that community's story. Published in 1996, it spent 10 weeks on the Chicago Tribune's best-seller list.

- The authoritative volume on Jewish participation in the Civil War is the imaginatively titled "American Jewry and the Civil War," by Bertram Korn. For more details on Edward Salomon, see my article, "From Immigrant to General in Ten Years," in the Winter, 1992 issue of "Chicago Jewish History."

- The most popular book on the Jews of the Lower East Side is Irving Howe's "World of Our Fathers." While it downplays religion and Zionism in favor of socialism and Yiddishism, it is still an excellent and readable work.

- The growth of the different religious streams among American Jewry can be seen from the perspective of either the synagogue or the rabbinate in the following two books respectively: "The American Synagogue: A Sanctuary Transformed," edited by Jack Wertheimer, and "The American Rabbinate, 1883-1983," edited by Jacob Marcus (who else?) and Abraham Peck. Yeshiva University is chronicled in three separate books: "The Story of Yeshiva University" (another inspired title), by Gilbert Klaperman, "The Men and Women of Yeshiva," by Jeffrey Gurock, noted history professor who also served as assistant coach of YU's basketball team, the Maccabees, and "Bernard Revel: Builder of American Orthodoxy," by my rebbe and teacher, Aaron Rakeffet-Rothkoff.

- The pre-Israel history of American Zionism is found in Melvin Urofsky's "American Zionism from Herzl to the Holocaust." Ted Berkman told the Mickey Marcus story in "Cast a Giant Shadow," which became the movie by the same name.

- America's lack of action during the Holocaust is analyzed with passion in David Wyman's "The Abandonment of the Jews." Another good book in the topic is "The Politics of Rescue," by Henry Feingold (a very diligent fellow, I must say). The tepid U.S. welcome to survivors of the Holocaust is examined in "America and the Survivors of the Holocaust," by Leonard Dinnerstein.

- Dinnerstein's "Anti-Semitism in American History" is the best of several histories of that subject.

- The current state of affairs between Jewish-Americans and African-Americans is discussed by Jonathan Kaufman in "Broken Alliance: The Turbulent Times Between Blacks and Jews in America." The title says it all.

- The Jews who created Hollywood are profiled in Neal Gabler's fascinating book, "A World of Their Own." Unfortunately, those Hollywood Jews, who were fleeing their identity, created a Judenrein America on the screen.

- Jewish gangsters are discussed in "But He Was Good to His Mother," by Robert Rockaway, a rare example of a Jewish history book with a catchy title (though, I'd expect a man named Rockaway to be creative).

- Two excellent books document the lives of Holocaust survivors in America: "New Lives," by Dorothy Rabinowitz, which appeared in 1976, and "Against All Odds: Holocaust Survivors and the Successful Lives They Made in America," by another fellow YU alumnus, William Helmreich, which was published in 1992. Helmreich's thesis is that despite the sufferings they endured, the vast majority of Holocaust survivors have made normal, stable, and successful lives for themselves in the United States, a fact that I always knew from first-hand observation. The classic, though dated, work on children of Holocaust survivors is Helen Epstein's "Children of the Holocaust."

- Combining the tales of both survivors and their children are "Maus" and "Maus II," by Art Spiegelman. Spiegelman told his father's Holocaust story in the form of a comic book, with the Jews as mice, the

Germans as cats, etc. The scenes shift from 1940s Poland to 1970s America, as we see the underlying tension between Art and his father. Despite the fact that the Spiegelman family is more dysfunctional than most (and proves the Lottie Gleicher Rule), "Maus" is one of the most important recent works on American Jewish history, and is even available in an expanded CD-ROM version.

- What does it mean to live as a Jew in America today? Four books, representing three different generations, attempt to explore that issue. The first is "Inside, Outside," by Herman Wouk. This semi-autobiographical work is strongest when profiling the hero's early life in the Bronx. Wouk shifts between New York in the '20s and '30s, and Washington in the '70s to illustrate the change in Jewish life in America over those years.

- Controversial as ever, Alan Dershowitz, in "Chutzpah," is the very model of the proud Jew. Sure, he started off his legal career representing leftists of all stripes, and not caring about Jewish causes, but he's since learned his lesson, and uses money from Leona Helmsley and Claus von Bulow to pay for defending Jonathan Pollard.

- One generation further, Ari Goldman, former religion reporter for the New York Times, wrote the introspective book, "The Search For God at Harvard." Goldman describes the conflicts of being religiously-observant in today's America, and the compromises he feels he has had to make in his job with the Times. Goldman is a thoughtful and intelligent author, and I identified with much of what he wrote.

- Newest of these autobiographies is "Memoirs of a Jewish Extremist," by Yossi Klein Halevi of the Jerusalem Report (and formerly of Brooklyn). Klein is an excellent writer and his book describes perfectly the world of young modern Orthodox Jews and the attraction Meir Kahane had for many of them. As Siskel & Ebert would say, "Two thumbs way up."

- Zev Chafets, Klein's colleague at the Jerusalem Report, traveled through America some years ago, and produced, "Members of the Tribe," a fascinating look at the interesting fringes of American Jewish life. Robert Eisenberg describes the different worlds of Chassidim in "Boychiks in the Hood" (another great title).

- The best way to keep up with the American Jewish community is to get a subscription to Moment magazine. Under the editorial guidance of Hershel Shanks, Moment's timely and insightful articles have made it the best periodical on the American Jewish scene.

- Earlier, I described the huge amounts of money raised for Jewish causes. Only one work describes how that mysterious process really works: "Machers: Fundraising and Leadership in the Chicago Jewish Community," a fascinating 1993 Northwestern University Ph.D. thesis by Marc Jon Swatez.

- A more humorous description of American Jews today can be found by watching the videotapes of Jackie Mason's Broadway shows. Sure, it's comedy and exaggeration, but Mason reveals many truths as well. You'll find yourself (in between hysterics) thinking "He's describing people I know." In many ways, Jackie describes the Jewish community better than a shelf-full of sociology volumes.

- Finally, after gorging yourself on Jewish history, snuggle up with "The Big Book of Jewish Humor," by William Novak and Moshe Waldoks and "Jewish Humor" by Joseph Telushkin. Why? Because Jewish history isn't always funny; more often than not, it's tragic. But you can't go through life with a frown; you've got to laugh a little. With those two books, you'll laugh a lot. Remember, laughter produces endorphins and other good chemicals, and causes you to live longer. Who knows? Maybe Jacob Marcus's secret was that he was a closet Three Stooges fan.

INDEX